Coolmath™ Algebra

PART 2

----- > first edition < -----

by Karen Lyn Davis

Coolmath.com, Inc.

Coolmath Algebra: Part 2
First Edition

© 2007 Coolmath.com, Inc.

ISBN-13: 978-0-9791628-1-7
ISBN-10: 0-9791628-1-5

All inquiries should be addressed to:

Coolmath.com, Inc.
P.O. Box 4386
Costa Mesa, CA 92628-4386

http://www.coolmath.com

Printed in the U.S.A.

Teachers and home schooling parents, please read the next page to find out about fair use in the classroom.

Copyrights & Fair Use in the Classroom

First of all, thank you for taking the time to read this. I'm sure you're all aware of copyrights and their importance in protecting the work of the creators of unique and innovative educational materials such as Coolmath.com and Coolmath Algebra.

Fortunately, for teachers and students there is something called "fair use." Simply put, fair use is the exception that allows teachers and students to use (within some very restrictive guidelines) copyrighted materials for educational purposes in the classroom. I've found that many teachers are unaware of the specifics regarding fair use of copyrighted materials like websites. (I, too, was quite uninformed in this area until I started to do some investigating!)

For students, fair use is easy! Students can use graphics and content all they wish (without permission) as long as it is for a class assignment. The only restrictions are that the "borrowed" content cannot be displayed in a public forum such as a website without the permission of the copyright holder and the content cannot be put into a situation where it can be distributed or copied. Students cannot give the content to someone else for use... **Specifically, you cannot make copies of this book or any portion of this book for your friends.**

For teachers, it's a bit more complicated and MUCH more restricted. To cut to the chase, **the key is to never use anything that would cause the copyright owner to lose income.** For example, photocopying any portion of a textbook (or other book) for classroom use instead of buying copies of the book for each student. Or downloading or printing a portion of a website for classroom use instead of visiting the site "live" so that the publisher can receive the income from the online ads.

So, where does this put us with Coolmath Algebra? If you want to use Coolmath Algebra in the classroom, you have two options available:

1) Visit the Algebra area of Coolmath.com live in the classroom. **Coolmath.com, Inc. is granting you the right to use the WEBSITE Coolmath.com in the classroom as much as you'd like -- AS LONG AS YOU VISIT THE SITE LIVE!** You cannot print the lessons and you cannot download (or cache) the lessons onto your hard drive.

2) Purchase the appropriate amount of copies of this book for your students.

Please understand that we can only afford to continue to maintain our websites and create new and innovation learning materials if we can be reimbursed for our time and expense. The only ways we can be reimbursed are through the ads on our sites and the purchase of our books. Your assistance in this area is greatly appreciated!

How can you help support Coolmath? Please ask your school and your district to create links on their official websites to Coolmath.com (or any of our other sites). These links help our rankings with search engines such as Google. Higher rankings help new people find us... And helping as many people as possible is our goal!

For more information about copyrights and fair use, a good resource is from the Standford University Library:

http://fairuse.stanford.edu/Copyright_and_Fair_Use_Overview/index.html

Thanks for your interest in Coolmath... And thanks again for reading this. We really appreciate teachers like you!

Coolmath Algebra – Part 2
Table of Contents

YOUR MATH SURVIVAL GUIDE

QUADRATICS

COMPLEX NUMBERS

SYSTEMS OF EQUATIONS

FUNCTIONS AND INVERSE FUNCTIONS

EXPONENTIALS AND LOGARITHMS

THE BACK OF THE BOOK

YOUR MATH SURVIVAL GUIDE

I Was a Mathphobe!

Hey, I used to hate math and I even thought I was terrible at it! And now I'm one of the most famous math geeks on the planet... *There's* **something to brag about, Baby!**

Here's my story:

My only memory of math in elementary school is listening to a tape of a man saying, "Three times four is.... Four times four is... Five times four is... Blah blah blah." It was one of those drills where you had to write down the answers before he asked the next one. It just occurred to me... Why couldn't my teacher have asked us these questions? Why on earth did they need a tape for this?! Anyway, that's all I remember.

But, seventh grade – boy, do I remember seventh grade! Much to my chagrin, they stuck me in one of those "gifted" programs. You know the ones – where you have to do twice as much work as the other kids and get lower grades as a reward. This never did make sense to me. So, I was in something called 7X Math. I guess the "X" was put in there as some sort of sick algebra joke. It was a cruel irony to say the least. I remember this class very well and I remember being completely clueless the entire time. I also remember how it felt to have "F" exams passed back to me and seeing that everyone around me seemed to be getting A's and B's. How could these students understand all the hieroglyphics and cave drawings the teacher kept scribbling all over the board? I remember the teacher too... Oh... I remember him. Mr. Ubbernerd (not his real name). Unfortunately, our class was right after lunch. He always managed to have at least half a pound of white Weber's bread left in his front teeth. And there was this little blob of spit... As he talked, it would string from the middle of his upper lip to his lower... up... down... up... down. It was mesmerizing. Perhaps this is why I failed the class – spit blob obsession.

My next math teacher (I think it was the second half of seventh grade) was nice. I don't remember learning any math, particularly, but I do remember that it wasn't safe to sit in the front because he sprayed spit when he talked. (Do you see a "too much saliva" theme going on here too? What's with that?)

Now, on to eight grade – Prealgebra. I had math during 7th period and there was a kid named David in our class. I'm sure you had a kid like David in your grade. He was the kid that always orchestrated the dropping of books at exactly 2:15, the kid who knew how to convert a Bic pen into a pellet shooter and the kid who always had enough spit for 18 spit wads (all to be aimed at the classroom clock). That kid. My teacher hated that kid and the rest of the class along with him. So, between David and what seemed to be a chronic case of PMS on my teacher's part, I didn't learn any math that year.

Ninth grade – Prealgebra yet again. Does this mean that I failed 8th grade math? I think it does even though no one really said that at the time. This year went pretty well. I had a good teacher and I remember that I got some good grades. Things were looking up for me – mathematically speaking.

Then came tenth grade – Algebra 1. The teacher told us that we could either pay attention or sleep, just as long as we didn't talk. So, I slept. Hey, it was right before lunch and my blood sugar was dropping. I didn't do any homework yet I still, somehow, miraculously managed to squeak out C-'s on my tests – just barely enough. That was fine with me after what I'd been through.   I just wanted to get the heck out of there!

I spent the next several years successfully avoiding math at all costs. At one point, I thought about majoring in Chemistry. I had a fantastic chemistry teacher and you could mix wildly colored things and make them smoke. Fun stuff. So, I sent away for information from my two local state colleges… Ouch! They both said that I'd have to take two years of Calculus. TWO YEARS OF CALCULUS!! I figured that I'd never be able to get through that and dropped the idea. (By the way, I now TEACH Calculus.)

Then it happened. In the fall of 1985, I was forced (at gunpoint – I swear) by my college to take a math class. It was Intermediate Algebra. I had to eat three Rolaids just so I could look at the schedule to pick a class time. Over the years, I had grown to view math in the same way as things like cooties and the Ebola virus – avoidance at all cost! But, I wanted to go to college… and I hadn't taken enough math in high school (cootie avoidance)… So, I was stuck.

After two packs of Rolaids and some Imodium-AD, I finally picked the class – late morning, so I could sleep in, of course. Hey, I was a serious student!

I still remember that first class… I didn't know whether I was going to throw-up, pass out or start crying. The teacher kept saying, "… and you remember THIS from last semester…" Last semester… Last semester? I didn't take any math last semester! Oh my GOSH! I was supposed to take MATH last semester?!

I leaned over and whispered to the student next to me, "Last semester? Do you know what he's doing?" She quickly shook her head, "No." She had the same horrified look on her face as I did.

The teacher was in rare form that day, my friend – all hopped up on coffee and donuts and covered from head to toe with chalk dust... "And you remember this type of linear blah-blah whose graph is clearly blah blah blah..." "Clearly." Uh... Yeah. Good thing I had the Rolaids with me. This guy was a major grouch who obviously had some sort of deficient childhood. Yes, he had scared the living crud out of me.

After class, the other clueless student and I cautiously approached the teacher – much like one would approach a live grenade or a baby that was accidentally fed chili. We got up our nerve and told him that neither of us had taken any math the previous semester and that we didn't recognize anything he had just done on the chalkboard. He gruffly told us that we'd never be able to pass his class and that we should drop and take an easier one. He wasn't exactly kind about it. I think his exact response was, "You're going to fail this class. Get out!"

Boy, were we mad! We got out in the hallway and agreed that he wasn't going to chase US off! We were going to show HIM! The nerve of that guy! Luckily, we decided to NOT try to run him over in the parking lot. Hey, things like that have consequences!

We studied and studied... And we both got A's on the first test! To this day, I'll never forget having that "93" paper handed back to me. I can still picture it. Boy, what a great feeling that was.

So, after a LOT of hard work, I ended up getting a B in that class. (I would have gotten an A, but after ripping a 93% on the first test, I got cocky and didn't study for the second one... I ate a big D- that day and learned a big lesson!)

But, do you really know what I learned that semester? Math wasn't so bad after all. In fact, it was pretty fun! I guess I had really never given it a chance. Heck, who would have guessed that I could be really good at it?

By the way, that grumpy professor turned out to be a really nice guy who gave me a lot of extra help. He even talked me into becoming a college math teacher. And that other initially clueless student turned out to be the best study-buddy anyone could ask for. She got an A that semester and is now a high school math teacher.

It just goes to show you... You never know where you'll end up. ANYTHING can happen. You might even end up LIKING math! But, don't worry... I'm not going to try to turn you into a math major! Let's just get you through this so you can go on to live a happy life.

Do You Hate Math?
Or Are You Just Afraid of It?

Hate or afraid – it's kind of the same thing.

I hate spiders… Why? Because I'm afraid of them. It doesn't matter that without spiders the world would be covered with bugs. I don't care about that. I hate them anyway. They're creepy and have thick, hairy legs. When I see one, it's him or me – I go into attack mode. The way I see it, if he's really big and I don't kill him, I'll have to move out of my house… Because I'll know he's in there… somewhere… waiting to kill me in my sleep… taunting me… and making baby spiders.

Last year, I actually saw a spider who only had three legs – one on the left (his left, not mine) and two on the right. I let him live. Hey, any spider who had survived a tragedy that ripped 5 legs off (or worse – five individual traumas each taking one leg), had really earned the right to live. That spider was a miracle! So, I let him get away – albeit, very slowly.

What was I talking about? Oh, yeah… math! Hate or fear: the result is the same – when you see a math book, you scream and jump onto the nearest chair. Wait… That's me with spiders. How about this? You get sick to your stomach and develop a nervous twitch in your left eye while little beads of sweat sprout on your upper lip.

I know. I was there. I hated math. I thought I was terrible at it too. So, I know how you feel. I know how it feels to stare at a chalkboard full of math that may as well be in a foreign language. I know how it feels to sit and stare at a page full of math problems and not even be able to do the first one. I know how it feels to be so overwhelmed and frustrated that tears start flowing. I know.

But, it may not be that you hate math… and it may not be that you are afraid of math… It may just be that you think you stink at math! Keep reading…

Think You Stink at Math?

Do you think you're bad in math? If you're reading this page, I'll bet you do. It's also a good bet that it someone **told** you that you're bad at math.

Most people can think of one thing, one incident, one terrible haunting memory that has made them think they stink at this stuff. If this is you, take a minute and write down what happened and how it made you feel. Here's an empty spot. (I'll wait.)

So, you think you're bad in math? Well, guess what? You're wrong! DEAD WRONG! And, if someone told you that you are bad in math, *they* were wrong! DEAD WRONG!

You're NOT bad in math -- You just haven't done well in math in the past. It's doesn't mean you can't do it. It doesn't mean that you aren't good at it!

Grab a piece of paper and write this down... Go on! I'll wait:

It's not that I'm bad in math, it's just that I've had bad experiences with math!

Now, put that piece of paper in the front of your math notebook and look at it everyday before math class until you really believe it!

You are in good company with people who've been told that they stink at stuff.

Check out this list:

- **Albert Einstein** was four years old before he could speak and seven before he could read.

- As a boy **Thomas Edison** was told by his teachers that he was too stupid to learn anything.

- **Werner von Braun**, one of our most important rocket scientists from 1930 to 1970, flunked ninth-grade algebra. (Do you KNOW how much algebra you need to know to do rocket science? Dang!)

- **Winston Churchill** failed the sixth grade.

- **Leo Tolstoy**, author of War and Peace, flunked out of college.

- **Louis Pasteur** was rated mediocre in chemistry when he attended the Royal College. He went on to discover that "germs" cause disease prompting hospitals to start sanitizing things. He also invented milk pasteurization and cured rabies. (Yeah, he was mediocre, alright. Clearly, pretty lazy too. He only changed the world.)

- **Walt Disney** was fired by a newspaper editor because he had "no good ideas." (Yeah, Disneyland and animated cartoons were really bad ideas.)

- **Gwendolyn Sykes**, the Chief Financial Officer of NASA, failed Algebra! Now, she's in charge of the finances for one of the biggest companies around.

- **Paul Orfalea**, founder of Kinkos, was labeled as "retarded" in elementary school. He isn't, of course. He is dyslexic though, but he doesn't let that stop him.

- **Robert Kiyosaki**, author of the all-time best selling personal finance book, *Rich Dad, Poor Dad*, failed English twice in high school.

I wouldn't exactly put myself on the same list as the people above, but I failed Algebra too and now I'm a semi-famous math geek and make my living teaching the stuff.

So, put all the negative crud that someone else attached to you far behind you… It's time to move on to SUCCESS! **You CAN do it and you WILL do it.** It's just going to take some hard work and a positive attitude.

Do You Want to be Successful?

Of course you do! And I'm not talking about just being successful in your math classes. I'm talking about being a successful person IN EVERYTHING! So, do you want to be successful?

You may think that this was a silly question. No one daydreams about being unsuccessful. Let's see… I'm hoping to barely get by, live pay check to pay check and have a job I don't like and be, generally, unhappy. No way! No one really thinks that… But, it happens to people anyway… All the time.

This may be the most important thing I say in the whole book…

Having success is a decision we can make for ourselves.

Let's take a minute… I want you to write down your dream. What are you dreaming of? What are you striving for? Is it your dream job? Is it your dream house? What do you want for your future? And I want you to aim high! If you aim for the sky and only make it 80% of the way, it will still be a lot higher than if you started by aiming for mediocrity.

I'll wait while you write down your dream… Here's a blank spot to do it in…

My dream:

Read it 5 times – read it out loud. Then, close your eyes for 5 minutes and think about it. Visualize it!

Now, I'm going to tell you how you can get it. (By the way, if you're thinking, "Hey, this isn't talking about algebra." Yes, it is! Just wait.)

Highly successful people have 6 things:

- **Creativity**

- **The ability to think and figure things out**

- **The ability to self-teach**

- **Confidence**

- **A positive attitude**

- **DRIVE!**

Let's look at each one.

1) Creativity

When most people think of creativity, they think of artists, dancers and writers… But, the most successful people in business, engineering, science and medicine are highly creative! When Donald Trump is putting together a deal, he's got to be able to think out of the box. He even wrote the bestselling business book of all time called "The Art of the Deal." And what does it take to create something new in science? That's right… Creativity!

2) The ability to think and figure things out

Thinking and figuring things out isn't just for science and business. Working out a dance routine requires planning and thinking. Writing takes a LOT of thinking. In fact, everything that you would consider an "art" takes thinking and planning.

Whether it's a science, an art, business or something else, having both creativity and the ability to think and figure things out makes for a killer combination. But, this isn't all that's needed to be successful... You still need more!

3) The ability to self-teach

When you're close to the top or at the top, there's no longer anyone around to teach you what you need to know next. Those who make it to the top and stay there are the ones who figure out what they need to learn next and learn it on their own. This is especially true for someone setting out to create something that's never been done before!

Also, it will be very important, no matter what your first "real" job ends up being, that you be able to learn things quickly and, yes, even on your own. Suppose two people are hired at the same time for the same type of job. Both are supplied with the same introductory information to perform his/her job. Person #1 keeps bothering the boss asking question after question. Person #2 carefully reviews the materials provided and starts working - perhaps just asking a couple of thoughtful and intelligent questions. If you were the boss, which new employee would impress you the most?

Of course, asking questions is often very necessary, but you'll want to try to find the answer on your own before asking. The last thing you want your boss to say is, "That's on page 2 of your instruction package." Then you look like a royal doofus – something to be avoided at a new job. Don't say I never gave you any good advice. Avoid looking like a royal doofus.

4) Confidence

You may have it or you may not. You may have it in some areas and not in others. It sure seems like some people were just born confident. You see them walking around school acting like they've got it all together. In reality, they're probably just better at ACTING confident and, on the inside, they may feel differently. The great thing is that confidence can be built from items 1, 2 and 3 above!

5) A positive attitude

Have you ever heard the phrase "Bloom where you are planted?" No? OK, pretend that you're a little flower seed getting blown down an old paved road... You fall in a crack. Well, dang it, BLOOM ANYWAY! Of course, it would have been nice to have been planted in a nice pot with nutritious soil just the right amount of water... But, you got stuck with a crack in the road, so make the most of it!

I'm sure that a math class is not where you'd like to be spending your time. But, you don't have much of a choice in the matter, do you? You may really like the idea of being in school and learning... But not THIS stuff!

There comes a time in life when you have to decide what kind of person you are going to be. Are you the type that will gripe and complain the whole time? Or are you the type that will make the best of the situation and find a way to use it to your benefit?

Successful people are always the ones to look at a seemingly unpleasant situation or a bad turn of events and say, "How am I going to use this to my advantage?" They will always find a way to make the most out of everything.

When life gives you lemons, make lemonade – AND SELL IT!

6) Drive

Highly successful people set their goals... and they aim high. They know what they want and they go after it. They want it badly and are willing to work very hard to get it!

Six things... That's it.

Now, let's focus on your attitude...

So, you're stuck taking a class and having to learn stuff that you, most likely, will never need. Why do you have to even take this class?! I mean, it's all SO unfair! This crud is standing between you and your dreams!

Well, everyone on the planet has decided that you need a certain amount of math to get out of high school and that you need a certain amount of math to get a college degree. That's the deal. Why do you think this is? Is it because you'll need math for your job? Not likely. So what is it?

Math trains you to think… and to figure things out.

OK, so you say you've heard THAT line before… and you're not buying it.

You want to be a successful person, right? A successful person would figure out a way to use a class like this to his or her advantage. A successful person would want to take this seemingly bad situation and twist it around. A successful person would take these lemons, make lemonade AND SELL IT! And YOU are going to be a successful person!

So, here's the silver bullet – the secret to success – the key to surviving this algebra thing:

It's not about the math!

You're not in a math class!

THIS IS A CLASS IN SUCCESS TRAINING!

You're going to use your algebra class to learn how to be successful. You're going to learn how to be creative, how to think and figure things out and how to self-teach (this is the most important one). It just so happens that the subject you're going to use to learn these things is Algebra.

The confidence will come quickly as you conquer this algebra stuff. Hey, if you can learn this, you can learn ANYTHING. You'll attack the rest of your classes and rip A's. Nothing will scare you anymore (except, maybe, spiders).

The positive attitude and the drive are up to you. These are things that have to come from deep inside YOU! These are your decisions… All you have to do is to decide to have them and they are yours… and no one can take them away! These are the two most important things to get you started.

I know you're still skeptical at this point, but bear with me… and trust me. I've taken thousands of mathphobes worse than you and turned them into savage algebra animals who can rip through the most treacherous of algebra exams with relative ease!

You can do this!

How to be a Successful Student

1) Always attend the first class meeting! This lets you know what the teacher is like and what is expected of you.

2) Read the class syllabus! (Or whatever the teacher passes out the first week) This will let you know all the rules regarding absences, exams, etc.

3) Be on time for class! In fact, always try to be a little early, so you can get out all your stuff.

4) Don't miss class unless you are really sick (nobody wants your germs!). Your teacher can explain something to you in a fraction of the time that it would take you to figure it out on your own (or even with the help of a tutor.)

5) If you do have to miss a class, always call a classmate (before you return to class!) to find out what you missed and if your teacher assigned anything that will be due when you return.

6) During class, always have your calculator on your desk and have your text book out. Teachers often do problems out of the book as examples.

7) If the teacher is making some sort of computation, work along with him/her.

8) Take very neat class notes. Write down everything the teacher writes down and try to write down most of what he/she says. Put stars by problems or points that your teacher stresses or get excited about. These are good potential exam questions!

9) Participate and ask questions!

10) Do your homework the same day that you hear the lecture on the material! If that isn't possible, always be sure to do the homework before you go to the next class.

11) Make friends in the class and study with them! I.E. Form well-balanced study groups. A good study group consists of 4 or 5 students with a range of capabilities. (Students getting D's and F's should never study together - This doesn't benefit anybody. It just turns out to be a big pity party.)

12) The second that you start to feel overwhelmed with the material (ex: you didn't understand a thing the teacher said or you can't do the assignment that night) get help! Go to your math learning center, get a tutor, ask for help from a classmate and go to your teacher's office!!

13) Get in the proper frame of mind! This class is your job. How much effort are you putting forth? Do you always clock in late or do you just not show up? If this class was *really* your job, would you get fired or would you be up for a raise?

How to Study for a Math Test

When studying for an algebra test, you have two main goals:

- Learn the material so you can do well on the exam.

- Learn the material well enough so you will still know it next semester!!! (Most of you will be taking more math. These classes ALWAYS depend on the material you learned the previous semester! If you don't really learn it (i.e. not just cramming for the exam), you'll crash and burn in your next class!

Tip #1:
Have all memorizing done *a couple of days before the exam... BUT, you should UNDERSTAND what's going on! Trying to just memorize it never lasts.*

Tip #2:
USE FLASH CARDS FOR MEMORIZATION OF FORMULAS AND RULES!!!

---

1) Starting out:

- Look over lecture notes.
    - REWORK EXAMPLES!!
- Look over homework.

2) Make an exam for yourself (or better yet, for a study partner):

- Take it after a delay period - So you won't remember where you got the problems - If you take the exam too soon, you may think you know the material better then you do! (*This should be done at least TWO (2) days before the exam - NOT the night before or you'll freak yourself out!*)

NOTE: It is extremely important that you be able to do the problems _without_ knowing what section they came out of!! Be sure to mix the problems up when you are practicing!

---

3) Restudy:

- Go back over what you had trouble with on your practice exam. This is the stuff that you didn't absorb well enough from just doing your homework.

4) The afternoon before exam day:

- *Read through your lecture notes and think!* Work some problems and review memorizing.

5) The night before exam day:

- Do something fun ----------- But not *too* much fun! 8-)

6) One hour before exam:

- Glance over flash cards and don't talk to classmates -- They may say something to confuse you or make you nervous. 8-)

Above all → DON'T CRAM!!!

Anything you try to learn at the last minute (that means the night before) will dribble out your left ear when you get nervous!

Dealing with Anxiety

Most students experience anxiety over math tests. It's normal. In fact, studies show that you should be a bit anxious before and during exams because it makes you perform better. So, a little anxiety is a good thing. What isn't good is when the anxiety gets so bad that it gives you a sick stomach and makes you cry! This level of anxiety can interfere with your performance. As you'll read later, I don't think a case of nerves can drop an A student down to an F, but I do think it can drop you to a B or C based on nervous mistakes like 2 x 3 = 5 or dropping a negative sign.

The only students who don't have even a little test anxiety are the ones who know they're going to fail and don't care.

Heck, I've even had test anxiety! I'm sure you can only imagine how many math tests I've had to take in my lifetime. I've been through the gambit of anxieties... the sleepless night, the upset stomach, the headache, the stiff neck, the tears... It wasn't pretty stuff.

But, I learned a very important lesson one day. I had three upper division (college) math classes one semester (actually, most semesters), so I had three math finals in one week to look forward to. Of course, I had studied well for all of them, but by the end of the second one, I was fried! My brain was cooked. I was so completely over the whole thing. While I was leaving campus after final exam #2, I ran into the professor who was giving final exam #3 the next day. He smiled and asked me if I was ready for his final. I looked at him and said, "Right now, I'm so tired that I don't even care."

I went home, studied a bit more and slept. The next morning I was still fried – sleep hadn't helped. I dragged myself over to school for the last final exam... and, really, I was too tired to care how I did! That was a first for me. I'd always been really competitive with myself about my math grades. (Can you say "geek"?) That day, I was too tired to care... and it was the very first math test I'd taken where I wasn't the least bit nervous! It was great. I just calmly sat there and easily worked the problems -- a snap. In fact, I got a perfect paper... and one of those problems was a killer! But, I figured it out.

After that, tests weren't that bad... I realized that I didn't have to get myself all worked up over them.

But, then came my thesis defense! For my master's degree in math, I had to write a thesis. This was, basically, a 117 page book that contained a 63 page proof. (Geek!) The other 54 pages contained my explanations of the math used in the proof. It took me about 8 months to write it and it had to be accepted or I wasn't going to get my degree. So, this was a BIG deal. For the thesis "defense" I had to present and explain the proof to a group of 17 people: 12 professors (with PhD's) and 5 other graduate students... After, they got to ask questions and I had to know the answers. The whole thing was to take about an hour. Man, was I nervous!! In fact, I had been nervous about the defense for the last EIGHT MONTHS!

I'll never forget something that happened while I was driving over to school that morning... It suddenly occurred to me... I was going to have to do the defense no matter what... And I could do it while being nervous... Or I could do it while being calm. Either way, it was going to happen! I realized that I had a choice: be nervous or be calm... Calm would be so much more pleasant. So, I instantly calmed down and stayed that way the entire time. It was amazing. Just a simple decision and it worked!

You can make the same decision when you're taking math tests! I know that this may not seem like an easy thing for you though, so here are some exercises you can do that will help. Just like anything else, learning to be calm will take practice. The more you do these, the better you'll get! The most important thing for you to realize is that there IS something you can do to reduce your math anxiety.

Before tests (especially the night before) and while studying:

Visualization

Effectively using visualization is a two-parter: the first way is for relaxation and the second is in preparing for the future.

Let's first talk about visualization for relaxation. This can be a quickie thing that you do in your classroom right before a test, or the night before the test, or while you're waiting in line somewhere, or while you're sitting in a traffic jam... Or it can be done much like meditation where you are sitting or lying in a quiet place.

Close your eyes (unless, of course, you are driving -- or trying to read this) and picture yourself in a beautiful nature setting like the beach, the mountains or a meadow full of flowers. My favorite place is the beach and it's my book, so let's go there!

Visualize, smell, hear and feel every part of it. You're sitting on the warm sand with your shoes off... You can feel the warm sand between your toes... You are looking out at the waves as they break on the shore... Hear that soft, crashing sound of the surf and the seagulls... Feel the cool breeze hitting your face... Pick up a handful of warm sand and feel it slowly sift out between your fingers... Smell the clean, salty ocean air... This is a safe place... No cares... No worries... Just you and the beach... Peaceful... Relaxing... Feel the stress drain out of you as you soak up the warmth of the sand and the smell of the cool air...

Now that you've read it, try it yourself. Read it back through one more time... Then, close your eyes and try it...

Now, let's talk about visualization for success. This will best be done during quick study breaks, the night before a test and while you're driving and/or walking to class to take the test. Definitely combine it with your visualization for relaxation – either before or after, whatever is best for you.

Close your eyes... Picture yourself taking the math test... Sitting in your seat in the classroom... You're very calm and working the problems without anxiety... Your mind is clear and working at its best... You are remembering everything you studied... Picture yourself successfully working the types of problems you'll be getting... After you've completed the exam, picture a big red "A" and "Great job!" written at the top of the first page.

Relaxation Exercises

Sometimes it takes a lot of practice to learn how to relax, especially if you are a stressed out student. You probably don't even realize that the muscles in your back, neck and shoulders are all knotted up. The following are all exercises that will help you relax -- some are more time-consuming and some are quick things you can do while driving or before an exam. Work these into your daily routine and practice, practice, practice.

Head to Toe Inventory
This exercise is a great thing to do when you have 20 minutes or so, like before bedtime or when you are taking a study break. Lay on a bed or somewhere else that's really comfortable or sit up straight in a comfy chair. Put on some nice soothing music (something without vocals is best) or one of those "nature sounds" CDs or just have it quiet. If "quiet" in your house is impossible, get some earplugs.

What you're going to be doing is working your way through all the major muscle groups in your body -- first tightening them, then, letting them completely relax.

Here's the order...

Your face... your neck... your shoulders... your arms... back to your shoulders and upper back... your torso (chest, abs, lower back)... your caboose... your legs... your feet.

Then, once you're all mushy and relaxed, just lay still and enjoy.

Get Heavy
This is another one that's good when you have 20 minutes or so to really relax. Lie down or sit somewhere comfortable (sit up straight). Again, make things quiet or put on some mellow "new age" music or "nature sounds."

Working from your feet up, you are going to concentrate on making parts of your body really heavy... and, when we are on an area, I want you to imagine all the blood in your body rushing to that area.

First, your legs... Imagine all the blood in your body rushing to your legs and feel them get heavier and heavier. Don't push on them or move them at all. You can't move them, they are too heavy. When you feel the heaviness and the warmth of the blood rushing through them, move on... Next comes your core (your torso)... Then, your arms... When your body is heavy, imagine your head feeling cool and refreshed. Imagine a cool breeze blowing across your forehead and through your hair. Just lay and enjoy.

Take a 4 Count
This one is really simple and can be done anywhere even for just a minute or so and even DURING an exam... If you can't do a problem and start to freak out, this is a great one! Close your eyes (unless you're driving, silly!)... Slowly breathe in and count 1... 2... 3... 4... Now, slowly exhale and count 4... 3... 2... 1... Do this at a pace that you're comfortable with -- you don't want to hyperventilate! Don't let your mind wander. Concentrate on those numbers.

Good In, Bad Out
This one is very similar to "Take a 4 Count," but this one uses a bit of imagination. Again, you can do this one anywhere and for even just a brief time like during a test. Close your eyes (if you can)... Slowly breathe in and imagine that you are breathing in nothing but good stuff - positive thoughts, good things, pure air, relaxation... Now, slowly exhale and imagine that you are blowing out all your stress, bad thoughts, negativity, bad air. Again, don't hyperventilate! Don't let your mind wander. Concentrate on good in and bad out.

Or, you can just scream "serenity now" right in the middle of your math test! (Just kidding. That doesn't work and your math teacher probably won't appreciate it.)

Now, I have to say something tough here... and this is after seeing and talking to thousands of students over the years... Anxiety cannot take a student who really knows the material and make him/her completely fail a test. I've talked to MANY students who, upon receiving an F on a test, tell me that they "really knew the material" but just got nervous and blanked out. After doing a little digging, it always turns out that they really didn't know the material as well as they thought they did. The problem mostly occurs because students will look over their notes and see that it all looks very familiar... So, they make the assumption that they know the stuff. But, looking at completed problems is very different than looking at a bunch of questions that aren't in the same order as the sections in the book and be able to work them cold.

A case of nerves cannot drop an A or B student (one who really knows the stuff) down to an F. But, it can drop you a grade or two via a bunch of little arithmetic mistakes and things like dropping negative signs.

BUT... know this:
If you are taking a math test and you HAVEN'T studied as much as you should have, you SHOULD be nervous... In fact, if you haven't studied enough, I WANT you to be nervous and sick to your stomach! That's right. I want tears to start pouring. I want that test to be such a miserable experience for you that you will study your caboose off for the next one so you can do your best! I want the best for you and I want YOU to want the best for you too. You can't conquer math unless you try and try HARD! Make... it... happen!

READ THE WORDS!

That means, don't just look and the stuff with numbers and x's. **Read the words too!** Hey, I say some pretty important stuff with those words.

I know students. You're busy and you're impatient to just get this stuff. I've had thousands of my own students use this book… and I've had the opportunity to watch them read it during class. I learned pretty quickly that most students don't take the time to read the words. Oh, I'd get called over to answer a question… and the answer was in the paragraph on the page they just (supposedly) read. Busted!

But, don't worry. There really aren't that many words and none of them are that big (haha). It's not like a regular math book where you have huge paragraphs in 8 point font with dozens of long math words. It's just me… It'll be just like I'm talking to you in person. It'll be easy.

Read the words too and you'll get everything twice as fast. TRUST ME!

WRITE IN IT!

During each section, there will be spaces right on the page for you to try some problems for yourself… Write in the book! Don't do the work on a separate page. Do it in the book.

Why? OK, this is going to sound silly… The reason is because it psychologically merges you with the book and, thus, with the math. Yeah, I don't say goofy-psycho-babble stuff very often, but it's really true in this case. You will feel more connected with the book and with me if you work along and write in the spaces provided.

BACK UP!

Let's say that you're having troubles with finding the equation of a line that is perpendicular to another given line. (Sorry, I didn't mean to give you a headache so soon! Bear with me.) This kind of problem might not be your issue… It may be that you aren't comfortable with how to find the slope of a line (which is the first step). If you don't go back to learn that part properly, you've got no hope of doing the harder problem. So, be willing to back up a few sections (when you need to) and do some review. It will take a little more time at first, but it will pay off in the long run.

GO SLOWLY!

There are no prizes for who can read the math book the fastest. Take your time. As you read, really go slowly and always be thinking about what you are reading.

Follow along with my examples – don't just skim them. Take the time to follow each one of my steps.

It takes time to learn to do something really well. No one learns to play the piano overnight. It takes time and practice. **Be patient. You'll get it!!**

Why isn't this book typed? What's the matter, were you too cheap or too lazy to get it typed?

I get this question all the time, although not put quite so brutally… But, I know what they are thinking.

The answer is very simple! I remember what it was like to open up a math textbook and see all those graphs and all that little typed font… It always made me think, "This math was done by a machine and not by a person. I won't be able to do it." To me, math books always looked inhuman and impossible!

This book wasn't done by a machine… and it wasn't written by some math geek robot… It was written by me. It's just me explaining the stuff to you as if I was sitting right there next to you at your desk. It's human.

The answer to the follow-up question is "Yes, my hand hurt for a long time."

What's Coolmath?

Coolmath.com is a website that I started in the spring of 1997. Since then, I've added a ton of content and a bunch of other sites and we're currently helping about **100,000 students a DAY!**

I now have several other sites:

Coolmath4kids.com
Coolmath-Games.com
SpikesGameZone.com
ScienceMonster.com
FinanceFREAK.com
TotallyStressedOut.com

And I'm working on StudentSuccessWEB.com… But, it isn't up yet.

What are Karen's official qualifications?

Eh, this is the boring stuff. But, if you're interested... I have a BA and MS in Mathematics from California State University, Long Beach. I tutored many Algebra students while I was a student.

I stayed on as a teacher at CSULB and taught Algebra and Math for Elementary Teachers. Then, I got a full-time job at a local community college where I've taught just about everything from Algebra to Calculus. In total, I have 14 years of teaching experience. During the last five years, I've read a lot of books on the psychology of learning and even several business books on how to motivate people. Teaching is a lot more than just the math.

QUADRATICS

Quadratics - A Brief Intro

Actually, we've already been working with quadratics. They are the trinomial guys we've been factoring:

$$x^2 - x - 6$$

$$2y^2 - 8y - 10$$

What makes them quadratics is that they are 2nd degree polynomials. (They have a squared guy like x^2 or y^2.)

Now, we're going to be solving equations with them like

$$x^2 - x - 6 = 0$$

$$2y^2 - 8y - 10 = 0$$

Here's the big official form of a quadratic equation:

$$ax^2 + bx + c = 0$$

Where a, b and c are just regular numbers like 2, 3, $\frac{1}{5}$, 2.7, etc.

examples:

$$3x^2 - 4x + 2 = 0$$

$$a = 3 \qquad b = -4 \qquad c = 2$$

$$x^2 + 7x - 3 = 0$$

$$a = 1 \qquad b = 7 \qquad c = -3$$

$$5x^2 - x - 6 = 0$$

$$a = 5 \quad b = -1 \quad c = -6$$

$$3x^2 - 2 = 0$$

$$a = 3 \quad b = 0 \quad c = -2$$

$$-7x^2 + 5x = 0$$

$$a = -7 \quad b = 5 \quad c = 0$$

It would be silly to ever have $a=0$ in a quadratic -- Then we wouldn't have a squared guy!

Try it:

Find a, b and c: $\quad -3x^2 - x - 5 = 0$

_____

Find a, b and c: $\quad x^2 - 6 = 0$

_____

Also, the variable doesn't have to be x. It can be any letter. X is just our standard unknown variable guy.

So, what kind of answers will we get for these things?

Remember when you solved equations like this?

$$2x - 3 = 5$$

Solve it!

$$2x - 3 = 5$$
$$\underline{+3 \quad +3}$$
$$2x = 8$$
$$\frac{2x}{2} = \frac{8}{2}$$
$$x = 4$$

We always got <u>one</u> answer. Right?
What's the power on the x guy?

one!

$$2x - 3 = 5 \quad \longrightarrow \quad 2x^1 - 3 = 5$$

With quadratics, we've got a max power

of two.

$$x^2 - x - 6 = 0$$

So, we'll usually get two answers. You'll see.

This is a pretty easy method... But, it only works when you can factor something. As I told you before, except for in math books, things usually don't factor.

But, this is a good method to help you understand what's going on... So, here we go!

We're going to be using one basic idea for these:

$$\text{If } ab = 0$$
$$\text{then } a = 0 \text{ or } b = 0$$

Think about it! Let's go back to 2nd grade. Waaaaaay back...

Fill in the boxes:

$$4 \cdot \boxed{} = 0$$

$$\boxed{} \cdot 5 = 0$$

$$a \cdot \boxed{} = 0$$

$$\boxed{} \cdot b = 0$$

This idea will work for algebra blobs too:

If $(x-3)(x+2) = 0$

Either this blob must be 0...   or this blob must be 0.

So...   if $(x-3)(x+2) = 0$

then $(x-3) = 0$ or $(x+2) = 0$

Which is really just

$$x-3 = 0 \quad \text{or} \quad x+2 = 0$$

and we can easily solve these guys to get our answers:

$$x-3 = 0 \quad \text{or} \quad x+2 = 0$$
$$\underline{+3 \quad +3} \qquad \underline{-2 \quad -2}$$
$$x = 3 \qquad\qquad x = -2$$

Guess what? We just solved this guy:

$$x^2 - x - 6 = 0$$

Factor: $(x-3)(x+2) = 0$

Blobs = 0: $x-3 = 0$ or $x+2 = 0$

Solve:
$$\underline{+3 \quad +3} \qquad \underline{-2 \quad -2}$$
$$x = 3 \qquad\qquad x = -2$$

This "or" is kind of important since x cannot be 3 <u>and</u> -2 at the same time!

Do these answers both work in our original
equation? Let's check:

$$x = 3 : \qquad x^2 - x - 6 = 0$$

$$(3)^2 - (3) - 6 = 0$$

$$9 - 3 - 6 = 0 \quad \text{Yep!}$$

$$x = -2 : \qquad x^2 - x - 6 = 0$$

Remember, $\longrightarrow (-2)^2 - (-2) - 6 = 0$
these ( ) are
really important $\qquad 4 + 2 - 6 = 0 \quad \text{Yep!}$
for negative guys!

They both work, so they are both solutions to
the equation. They are really a set of solutions,
so we put them together in set brackets:

The official answer is $\{-2, 3\}$.

(No, this is NOT an (x,y) point like (-2,3.))

Let's do another one:

$$\text{Solve} \quad x^2 + 3x - 18 = 0$$

Factor: $(x - 3)(x + 6) = 0$

Blobs = 0: $x - 3 = 0 \quad \text{or} \quad x + 6 = 0$

Solve: $\underline{+3 \quad +3} \qquad \underline{-6 \quad -6}$

$$x = 3 \qquad \qquad x = -6$$

$$\{-6, 3\}$$

Try it:

Solve $x^2 + 8x + 12 = 0$

Remember how I said that since there's an

x^2 ← we hope to get
two answers?

Well, check out this guy:

Solve $x^2 + 4x + 4 = 0$

Factor: $(x+2)(x+2) = 0$

Blobs = 0: $x + 2 = 0$ or $x + 2 = 0$

Solve:
$$\frac{-2 \quad -2}{x = -2}$$
$$\frac{-2 \quad -2}{x = -2}$$

Hey! We got the same guy twice!

Don't worry. These are just Gilligan's Island
answers -- RERUNS!

So, the answer is just $\{-2\}$.

Try it:

Solve $x^2 - 6x + 9 = 0$

You've got the idea now. The factoring just gets messier.

Solve $3x^2 + 13x - 10 = 0$

Factor: $(3x-2)(x+5) = 0$

Blobs = 0: $3x - 2 = 0$ or $x + 5 = 0$

$$\underline{+2 \quad +2} \qquad \underline{-5 \quad -5}$$

$$3x = 2 \qquad\qquad x = -5$$

$$\frac{3x}{3} = \frac{2}{3}$$

$$x = \frac{2}{3}$$

$$\left\{-5, \frac{2}{3}\right\}$$

Your turn:

Solve $8x^2 - 26x - 7 = 0$

Sometimes, one of the pieces is missing... But, it's no big deal.

Check it out:

$$\text{Solve} \quad 3y^2 - 5y = 0$$

Factor:

$$y(3y - 5) = 0$$

Blobs = 0:

Solve:

$$y = 0 \quad \text{or} \quad 3y - 5 = 0$$

This guy's done.

$$\begin{array}{r} +5 \quad +5 \\ \hline 3y = 5 \end{array}$$

$$y = \frac{5}{3}$$

$$\left\{ 0, \frac{5}{3} \right\}$$

Your turn:

$$\text{Solve} \quad 4a^2 + 3a = 0$$

Here's another kind:

$$\text{Solve} \quad x^2 - 9 = 0$$

Remember the difference of two squares?

Factor:

$$(x - 3)(x + 3) = 0$$

Blobs = 0: $x - 3 = 0$ or $x + 3 = 0$

Solve: $\underline{+3 \quad +3}$ $\underline{-3 \quad -3}$

              $x = 3$ $x = -3$

                    $\{-3, 3\}$

Try it:

        Solve $x^2 - 25 = 0$

OK, let's take this one step further.

What if there were three blobs?

$$abc = 0$$

Back to 2nd grade -- fill in the boxes:

$$3 \cdot \square \cdot 6 = 0$$

$$\square \cdot 4 \cdot 2 = 0$$

$$8 \cdot 9 \cdot \square = 0$$

$$a \cdot \square \cdot c = 0$$

$$\square \cdot b \cdot c = 0$$

$$a \cdot b \cdot \square = 0$$

So... If $abc = 0$

then $a = 0$ or $b = 0$ or $c = 0$

(or all three are $= 0$)

Check it out:

Solve $\quad 2a^3 - 2a = 0$

Factor: $\quad 2a(a^2 - 1) = 0$

$\quad 2a(a-1)(a+1) = 0$

Blobs $= 0$:

$\quad 2a = 0 \quad$ or $\quad a - 1 = 0 \quad$ or $\quad a + 1 = 0$

Solve: $\quad \dfrac{2a}{2} = \dfrac{0}{2} \qquad \dfrac{+1 \ +1}{a = 1} \qquad \dfrac{-1 \ -1}{a = -1}$

$\quad a = 0$

$$\{-1, 0, 1\}$$

We started with a cubed guy: $2a^3 - 2a = 0$

and got three answers: $\{-1, 0, 1\}$

① ② ③

Try it:

Solve $\quad 5x^3 - 45x = 0$

Here's another one:

Solve $\quad x^3 + 2x^2 - 35x = 0$

Factor: $\qquad x(x^2 + 2x - 35) = 0$

$\qquad\qquad x(x-5)(x+7) = 0$

Blobs = 0:

Solve: $\quad x = 0 \quad$ or $\quad x - 5 = 0 \quad$ or $\quad x + 7 = 0$

done $\nearrow$ $\qquad\qquad \dfrac{+5 \;+5}{x = 5} \qquad \dfrac{-7 \;\;-7}{x = -7}$

$$\{-7, 0, 5\}$$

Your turn:

Solve $\quad 2y^3 + 5y^2 - 3y = 0$

We've been solving nice guys like

$$x^2 - 3x - 18 = 0$$

Notice that it's already set equal to 0.
So, what if the problem starts out like this?

$$x^2 - 3x = 18$$

Can we just factor and do the blob thing?

$$x(x-3) = 18$$

So $x = 18$ or $x - 3 = 18$

$$x = 21$$

Are these the answers? Check them!

$x = 18:$ $x^2 - 3x - 18 = 0$

$$(18)^2 - 3(18) - 18 = 0$$

$$324 - 54 - 18 = 0 \quad \text{No Way!}$$

Why didn't this work?
Think about our main idea:

$$\boxed{\text{If } ab = 0, \text{ then } a = 0 \text{ or } b = 0.}$$

IT MAKES SENSE!

But, THIS is what we tried:

If $ab = 18$, then $a = 18$ or $b = 18$.

WE CANNOT SAY THIS!

Uh... what about

$3 \cdot 6 = 18$ or $2 \cdot 9 = 18$?

There are a ton of things a and b can be other than 18.

So, when you start with something like

$$x^2 - 3x = 18$$

ALWAYS SET IT $= 0$ FIRST. ALWAYS!

$$x^2 - 3x - 18 = 0$$

Finish it!

Your turn:

Solve $x^2 + 7x = 170$

The other thing that can happen isn't super freaky... But, it will make your life a lot easier.

Let's say you're given this:

$$3 + 5x - 2x^2 = 0$$

Notice that the squared guy is negative. This makes factoring a really creepy experience. Remember... these guys are equations... So, all our old tricks work.

Can we multiply both sides by -1? Sure can, skippy! Do it!

$$-1 \cdot (3 + 5x - 2x^2) = 0 \cdot (-1)$$

$$-3 - 5x + 2x^2 = 0$$

Now, just rearrange it like you're used to:

$$2x^2 - 5x - 3 = 0$$

Finish it!

Try it:

Solve $11x + 6 - 10x^2 = 0$

One more thing: If you start with something like

$$12x = -2x^3 - 10x^2$$

Always move stuff around so your biggest power guy

$$12x = -2x^3 - 10x^2$$

is positive. Check it out:

$$12x = -2x^3 - 10x^2$$
$$+2x^3 + 10x^2 \qquad +2x^3 + 10x^2$$
$$\overline{}$$
$$2x^3 + 10x^2 + 12x = 0$$

Now, we can solve it!

Factor: $\quad 2x(x^2 + 5x + 6x) = 0$

$\qquad\qquad 2x(x+2)(x+3) = 0$

Blobs = 0:

$\qquad 2x = 0 \quad$ or $\quad x + 2 = 0 \quad$ or $\quad x + 3 = 0$

$\qquad\quad x = 0 \qquad\qquad x = -2 \qquad\qquad x = -3$

$$\{-3, -2, 0\}$$

Your turn:

$\qquad$ Solve $\quad -16x = -4x^3$

Quadratics - The Square Root Trick

You'll like this section. It's really easy!

Let's revisit those quadratics with no middle x guy... Like

$$x^2 - 4 = 0$$

There are two ways we can solve this guy:

WAY 1: our old factoring way:

$$x^2 - 4 = 0$$

$$(x-2)(x+2) = 0$$

$$x - 2 = 0 \quad \text{or} \quad x + 2 = 0$$

$$x = 2 \qquad\qquad x = -2$$

$$\{-2, 2\}$$

WAY 2: A new square root trick:

Let me explain it all, then you'll see that it's a really slick way to go.

$$x^2 - 4 = 0$$

First, get the x^2 alone:

$$x^2 - 4 = 0$$
$$\underline{+4 \qquad +4}$$
$$x^2 = 4$$

OK, here's the trick:

To "undo" this $\overset{\frown}{x^2}$

We'll take the square root: $\sqrt{x^2}$

Squares and square roots undo each other...
Right?

$$\sqrt{3^2} = \sqrt{9} = 3 \text{ Yep!}$$

$$\text{So, } \sqrt{x^2} = x$$

Now, remember our equation rules -- whatever
we do to one side, we have to do to the other.
So, we'll take the square root of both sides:

$$\sqrt{x^2} = \sqrt{4}$$

$$x = 2$$

Uh oh... We only got one answer. Hmm... We
got two answers when we factored.

$$x = -2 \text{ or } x = 2$$

Here's what you officially do to fix this problem:

$$x^2 = 4$$

$$\sqrt{x^2} = \pm\sqrt{4} \qquad \text{Put this } \pm \text{ in here!}$$

$$x = \pm 2$$

$$\{-2, 2\}$$

Here's another one done both ways:

$$x^2 - 81 = 0$$

WAY 1: factoring

$$x^2 - 81 = 0$$
$$(x-9)(x+9) = 0$$
$$x - 9 = 0 \text{ or } x + 9 = 0$$
$$x = 9 \qquad\qquad x = -9$$
$$\{-9, 9\}$$

WAY 2: square root trick

$$x^2 - 81 = 0$$
$$x^2 = 81$$
$$\sqrt{x^2} = \pm\sqrt{81}$$
$$x = \pm 9$$
$$\{-9, 9\}$$

Try it:

Solve $y^2 - 36 = 0$

WAY 1:

WAY 2:

OK, so if we can just factor these things, why do we need the square root trick? Ah, because sometimes you can't factor them! Check it out:

Solve $x^2 - 10 = 0$

Not the difference of two squares, is it?
So, we need the square root trick:

$$x^2 - 10 = 0$$

get the x^2 alone

$$\underline{+10 \quad +10}$$

$$x^2 = 10$$

$$\sqrt{x^2} = \pm\sqrt{10}$$

$$x = \pm\sqrt{10}$$

$$\{-\sqrt{10}, \sqrt{10}\}$$

Try it:

Solve $\quad a^2 - 3 = 0$

Here's a harder one:

Solve $\quad 25x^2 - 7 = 0$

get the x^2 alone

$$\underline{+7 \quad +7}$$

$$25x^2 = 7$$

$$\frac{25x^2}{25} = \frac{7}{25}$$

$$x^2 = \frac{7}{25}$$

$$\sqrt{x^2} = \pm\sqrt{\frac{7}{25}}$$

$$x = \pm\sqrt{\frac{7}{25}} = \pm\frac{\sqrt{7}}{\sqrt{25}} = \pm\frac{\sqrt{7}}{5}$$

$$\left\{ -\frac{\sqrt{7}}{5}, \frac{\sqrt{7}}{5} \right\}$$

Your turn:

Solve $8x^2 - 6 = 0$

There's a formula that will kill all quadratic equations... whether they factor or not... it will seek out and destroy... it will hunt down all solutions... It's...

THE QUADRANATOR!

Rumor is that this is going to be Arnold Schwarzenegger's next movie. He's going to go around giving everyone compound fractions. OK, here it is:

$$\text{If } ax^2 + bx + c = 0$$
$$\text{then} \quad x = \frac{-b \pm \sqrt{b^2 - 4ac}}{2a}$$

It's really calling the quadratic formula.

Know it... <u>LOVE IT!</u>

Now, I just need to show you what to do with it. That would be helpful, huh?

Let's do one we've done before so we'll recognize the answers when we get them:

$$2x^2 - 5x - 3 = 0$$
$$a = 2 \quad b = -5 \quad c = -3$$

Let's plug the stuff into our formula:

$$x = \frac{-b \pm \sqrt{b^2 - 4ac}}{2a} = \frac{-(-5) \pm \sqrt{(-5)^2 - 4(2)(-3)}}{2(2)}$$

$$= \frac{5 \pm \sqrt{25 + 24}}{4} = \frac{5 \pm \sqrt{49}}{4} = \frac{5 \pm 7}{4}$$

this is how we'll get our two answers!

One with the −:

$$x = \frac{5-7}{4} = \frac{-2}{4} = -\frac{1}{2}$$

One with the +:

$$x = \frac{5+7}{4} = \frac{12}{4} = 3$$

$$\left\{ -\frac{1}{2}, 3 \right\}$$

Hey, this is what we got before by factoring! So, this quadranator thing really works -- cool!

Try it:

Solve $60x^2 + 317x - 161 = 0$

Here's one that doesn't factor:

Solve $x^2 + x - 1 = 0$

$$a = 1 \quad b = 1 \quad c = -1$$

$$x = \frac{-b \pm \sqrt{b^2 - 4ac}}{2a} = \frac{-1 \pm \sqrt{(1)^2 - 4(1)(-1)}}{2(1)}$$

$$= \frac{-1 \pm \sqrt{1 + 4}}{2} = \frac{-1 \pm \sqrt{5}}{2}$$

$$\text{so} \quad x = \frac{-1 - \sqrt{5}}{2} \quad \text{or} \quad x = \frac{-1 + \sqrt{5}}{2}$$

Yep -- these messy little buggers are the answers:

$$\left\{ \frac{-1 - \sqrt{5}}{2}, \; \frac{-1 + \sqrt{5}}{2} \right\}$$

If you were in a science or business class, you'd need to pop these into your calculator to get decimal approximations for these. Since you may need to do this someday, we better practice this. Since all calculators are different, it won't do much good for me to tell you how to enter this in... So, you're on your own. Here are the answers:

$$\text{exact} \rightarrow \left\{ \frac{-1 - \sqrt{5}}{2}, \; \frac{-1 + \sqrt{5}}{2} \right\}$$

$$\text{decimal} \atop \text{approximation} \rightarrow \{ -1.618, \; .618 \}$$

* Find out which of these your teacher wants.

Here's another one:

$$2x^2 - 12x + 13 = 0$$

$$a = 2 \quad b = -12 \quad c = 13$$

$$x = \frac{-b \pm \sqrt{b^2 - 4ac}}{2a} = \frac{-(-12) \pm \sqrt{(-12)^2 - 4(2)(13)}}{2(2)}$$

$$= \frac{12 \pm \sqrt{144 - 104}}{4} = \frac{12 \pm \sqrt{40}}{4}$$

$$\text{exact} \rightarrow \left\{ \frac{12 - \sqrt{40}}{4}, \frac{12 + \sqrt{40}}{4} \right\}$$

$$\text{decimal approximation} \rightarrow \left\{ 1.419, \ 4.581 \right\}$$

Your turn:

Solve $x^2 + 7x + 2 = 0$

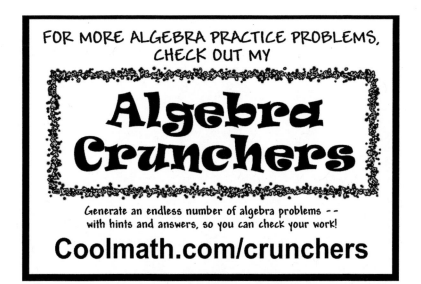

Quadratics - Solving Overview

We've got three methods for solving quadratics:

Method 1: factoring

* Quick and easy IF something factors right away ... only for math book problems.

example:

$$\text{Solve } 7x^2 - 22x + 3 = 0$$

Factor: $\quad (7x-1)(x-3) = 0$

Blobs = 0: $\quad 7x-1 = 0 \quad \text{or} \quad x-3 = 0$

$$7x = 1 \qquad\qquad x = 3$$

$$x = \frac{1}{7}$$

$$\left\{ \frac{1}{7}, 3 \right\}$$

Try it:

$$\text{Solve } 15x^2 + 26x + 8 = 0$$

Method 2:   Square Root Trick

*Works great when the middle x term is missing. Don't forget the $\pm$!

example:

$$\text{Solve } 4x^2 - 5 = 0$$

get x^2 alone:

$$4x^2 = 5$$

$$x^2 = \frac{5}{4}$$

$$\sqrt{x^2} = \pm\sqrt{\frac{5}{4}} = \pm\frac{\sqrt{5}}{\sqrt{4}} = \pm\frac{\sqrt{5}}{2}$$

$$\left\{ -\frac{\sqrt{5}}{2}, \frac{\sqrt{5}}{2} \right\}$$

Your turn:

$$\text{Solve } 9x^2 - 17 = 0$$

Method 3: The Quadranator

  * After a failed 10 second factor attempt, whack it with this and it will work every time. The problem is: If you forget the formula, you're dead meat.

$$ax^2 + bx + c = 0 \rightarrow x = \frac{-b \pm \sqrt{b^2 - 4ac}}{2a}$$

example:

Solve $3x^2 - 10x + 1 = 0$

$$x = \frac{-(-10) \pm \sqrt{(-10)^2 - 4(3)(1)}}{2(3)} = \frac{10 \pm \sqrt{100 - 12}}{6}$$

$$= \frac{10 \pm \sqrt{88}}{6}$$

exact $\rightarrow \left\{ \frac{10 - \sqrt{88}}{6}, \frac{10 + \sqrt{88}}{6} \right\}$

decimal approximation $\rightarrow \{.103, 3.230\}$

Try it:

Solve $2x^2 + 11x + 1 = 0$

Here are some problems to try. I'll help you with a plan of attack.

$$\text{Solve} \quad x^2 - 5x = 2$$

1️⃣ set it $=0$ first

2️⃣ 10 second factor attempt -- if it doesn't work, quadranate it

---

$$\text{Solve} \quad a^3 = a$$

1️⃣ set it $=0$ first (no, you cannot divide both sides

2️⃣ factor   by a... because $a=0$ is a solution!)

Solve $6x^3 + 12x^2 + 2x = 0$

① first rule of factoring (no, you cannot quadranate it in this form!)

② 10 second factor attempt → quadranator

Solve $b^2 - 7 = 0$

① square root trick

So far, we've only graphed lines... But, there are tons of other things out there to graph. (I know. This is all <u>very</u> exciting!) Quadratics have graphs called "parabolas."

Here's our most basic quadratic:

$$y = x^2$$

He's also our most basic parabola.
I call him Standard Parabola Guy!

Before I show you his graph, let's understand what Standard Parabola Guy does for a living:

He squares things!

He's a squaring machine, baby!
Things go in... and their squares spit out.
We feed x guys into the machine... and y guys spit out.
Let's feed the machine and this will give us the points to graph for Standard Parabola Guy...

inputs	the machine	outputs	point
x →	x^2	→ y	(x, y)
-2 →	$(-2)^2$	→ 4	$(-2, 4)$
-1 →	$(-1)^2$	→ 1	$(-1, 1)$
0 →	0^2	→ 0	$(0, 0)$
1 →	1^2	→ 1	$(1, 1)$
2 →	2^2	→ 4	$(2, 4)$

This gives us the set of points for
Standard Parabola Guy:

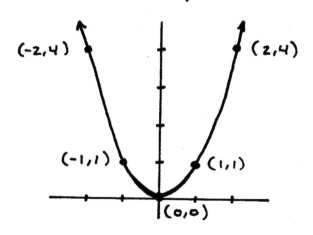

You need to learn this shape and know these points cold!

You are NOT going to need one of those x,y charts...

We only do this when we don't know the shape of something -- when we don't really know what we're doing!

From now on, we have a new motto:

PLOTTING POINTS IS FOR SISSIES!

The official Webster's dictionary definition of a "sissy" is a "weak or feeble person."

Who wants to be weak or feeble? NOT ME!

I want to be an algebra animal... a math monster...

A SUPER GEEK!

In the next sections, I'll show you how to graph all sorts of parabolas... and never once will we have to use one of those pathetic "plotting points" tables! We won't need to plot points, take stabs in the dark and make guesses... because we will be super genius graphers!

We're going to be moving Standard Parabola Guy around, so let's look at his basic shape again:

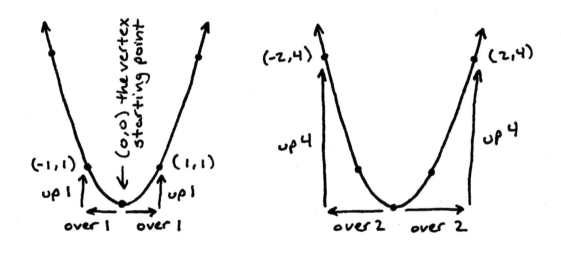

Remember that his job is to square things... What would the next set of points be?

over 3... square that... up 9

over 4... square that... up 16

Now that we know Standard Parabola Guy's graph... Wait a minute... I know it... But, do you really know it yet? NO PEEKING! Let's be sure before we go on.

Graph $y = x^2$ here... and no "plotting points." This is a sissy-free zone!

What's his job? _____

Remember, this will always help you graph him! Do it!

OK, now that we really do know the basic graph, we're going to learn how to shift him around.

First, we'll look at what happens when we have a number added onto the end of a parabola:

$$y = x^2 + 1$$

↑ This adds one to each of the outputs...
Those are the y guys!

So...

$y = x^2$

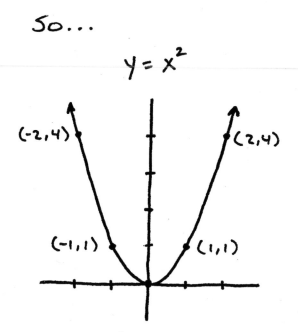

$y = x^2 + 1$

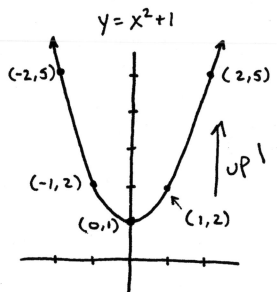

moves Standard Parabola Guy up 1

If we subtract a number off...

$$y = x^2 - 3$$

↑ This takes 3 off of each of the outputs (the y guys).

So...

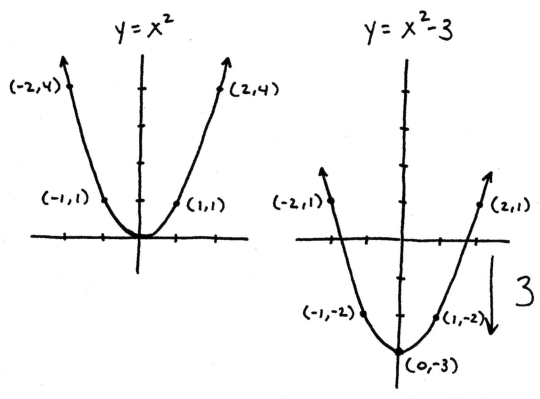

$y = x^2$ $\qquad$ $y = x^2 - 3$

(-2,4) $\qquad$ (2,4)

(-1,1) $\qquad$ (1,1)

(-2,1) $\qquad$ (2,1)

3

(-1,-2) $\qquad$ (1,-2)

(0,-3)

moves Standard
Parabola Guy down 3

Your turn:

Graph these and remember to identify what's
going on -- and not by plotting points. Be sure
to label 5 points like a polite math geek:

$y = x^2 + 2$

$$y = x^2 - 1$$

Let's sum up what we've got here:

When there's a number hanging off the end of Standard Parabola Guy...

It's a vertical shift!

$$y = x^2 + k$$

He moves up if k is positive.
He moves down if k is negative.

OK, so what if the extra thing on Standard Parabola Guy is inside some parenthesis with the x?

Like this guy:

$$y = (x-3)^2$$

First of all, is this thing still a parabola? Let's FOIL it:

$$y = (x-3)^2 = (x-3)(x-3) = x^2 - 6x + 9$$

There's an x^2 guy... So, yes!

What's going on with the graph of this thing?

$$y = (x-3)^2$$

Here's the game I play on these:

I pretend that this guy's whole goal in life is to be

$$y = (0)^2$$

That's all he wants!

What value of x will make him happy?

$$y = (x-3)^2 = (3-3)^2 = (0)^2$$
$$x = 3$$

So, we start him (i.e. put the vertex) over
at x = 3:

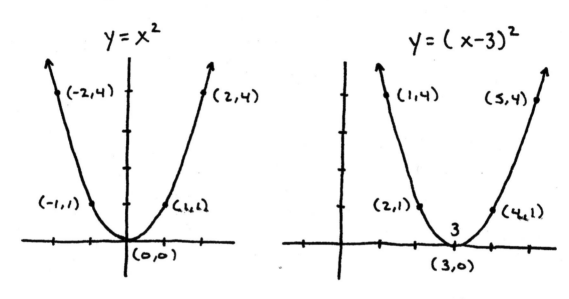

moves Standard
Parabola Guy over to
x = 3

What about this guy?

$$y = (x+2)^2$$

What will make him $y = (0)^2$?

$$y = (x + 2)^2$$
$$x = -2$$

So, start him over at $x = -2$:

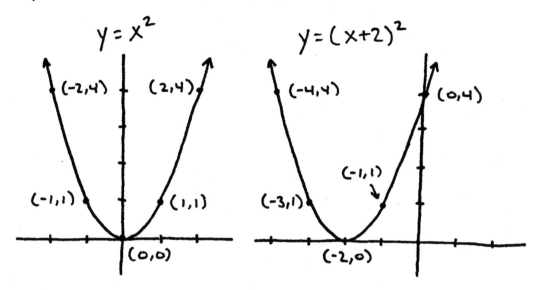

$y = x^2$

(-2,4)   (2,4)

(-1,1)   (1,1)

(0,0)

$y = (x+2)^2$

(-4,4)   (0,4)

(-1,1)

(-3,1)

(-2,0)

moves Standard Parabola
Guy over to $x = -2$

Try it:

Graph these and remember to identify
what's going on -- and not by plotting points.
Label 5 points!

$$y = (x-1)^2$$

$$y = (x+3)^2$$

Let's sum up what we've got here:

When there's a number INSIDE with the x guy:

It's a horizontal shift!

$$y = (x-h)^2$$

Find the x value that makes it
$(0)^2$ and shift it horizontally
to that spot.

* I always remember that, if the extra thing
  is inside with the x, then it effects x values--
  these move it back and forth along the x-axis.

Quadratics - Graphing Parabolas - Part 3

This one's a snap!

If Standard Parabola Guy is negative...

$$y = -x^2$$

Then, you flip him upsidedown!

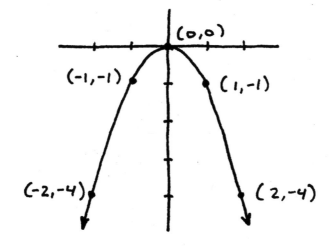

Quadratics - Graphing Parabolas - Part 4

So far, we've moved Standard Parabola Guy up and down... back and forth... and even flipped him upside down. All this time, he's kept his basic shape.

Ah... just when you started to feel really comfortable... Now, we're going to change his shape! Don't worry though. It's not that bad. Trust me. Have I lied to you yet? That you know of? (heh-heh)

He'll still have his "U" shape... We're just going to make him taller and shorter.

It will still be really important for us to keep his basic shape in our heads:

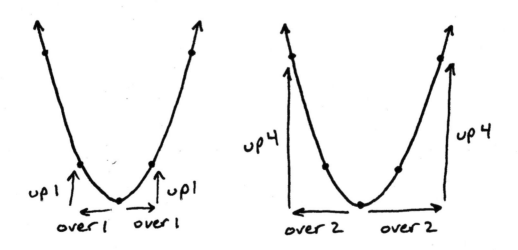

When you go over 1, you go <u>up 1</u>. That's how tall he is there.

When you go over 2, you go up 4. That's how tall he is there.

So, if we have this:

$$y = 2x^2$$

↑ This just means that he's twice as tall as normal.

(All the outputs are twice as big!)

When you draw him, just go up twice as far!

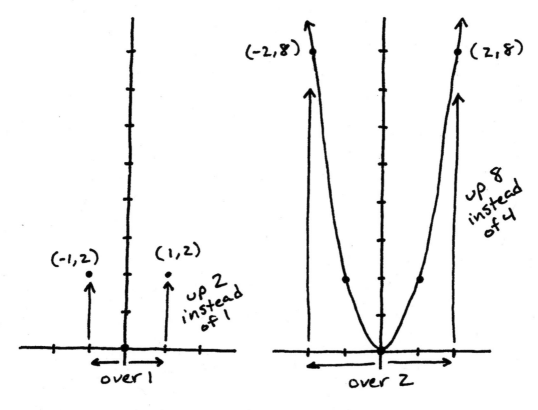

That wasn't that bad. The tricky part is drawing them so you don't get a "V" point down by the vertex. There's another graph that's a "V" shape, so be careful about this.

What about this guy?

$$y = \tfrac{1}{2} x^2$$

↑ This means that he's going to be half as tall as normal. (All the outputs are half as big!)

When you draw him, just go half way up!

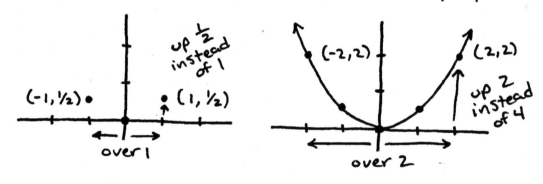

NOTE: If the textbook you're using uses the "wider" and "narrower" approach, it means the same thing. I just don't think it makes as much sense! But, they don't ask ME about these things!

Your turn:

Graph and identify what's going on -- don't plot points:

$y = 3x^2$ (label just 3 points)

_____

$y = \frac{1}{4}x^2$ (label 5 points)

_____

$y = 5x^2$ (label 3 points)

Let's sum up what we've got here:

When there's a number multiplied in front
of Standard Parabola Guy...

$$y = a x^2$$

If a is positive, then he's U.
If a is negative, then he's ∩.
The value of a makes him
taller of shorter.

Quadratics - Graphing Overview

We've got all the pieces, now let's put it together:

$$y = a(x-h)^2 + k$$

a: opens up or down
taller or shorter

h: the horizontal shift

k: the vertical shift

Let's do some graphing!

Here's our plan of attack:

① Identify what's going on. (and write it down)

② Do the shifting and set the vertex (the starting point).

③ Pretend you're at (0,0).

④ Deal with any flips or taller/shorter issues.

⑤ Label the points to be a polite math geek!

And remember...

PLOTTING POINTS IS FOR SISSIES!

Graph $y = -x^2 + 4$

$$y = \nearrow -x^2 + 4$$

$\wedge$ $\uparrow 4$

standard shape

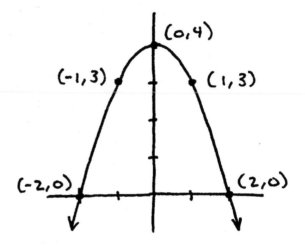

Graph $y = (x+2)^2 - 1$

$$y = (x+2)^2 - 1$$

$\nearrow$ $\downarrow 1$

$x = -2$

makes this

o^2

standard shape U

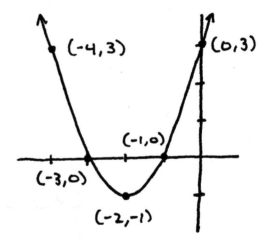

Graph $y = 2x^2 - 3$

$\nearrow$ $\downarrow 3$

twice as tall

U

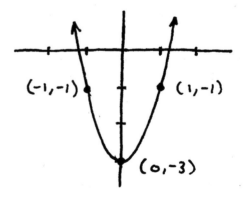

Try it:

$$y = -3x^2$$

$$y = (x+1)^2 - 4$$

$$y = 2(x-3)^2$$

$$y = (x-1)^2 + 2$$

Quadratics - Graphing by Completing the Square - Intro

As we saw in the previous lessons, when a parabola is in the form

$$y = a(x-h)^2 + k$$

it's pretty easy to graph.

The only problem is... they usually aren't in this form!

You might need to graph something like this:

$$y = -2x^2 + 4x + 1$$

Well, we can see by the $2x^2$ that this <u>is</u> a parabola... and that it will be upside down

$$y = -2x^2...$$

and twice as tall.

But, other than that, it's impossible to tell.

The "$+4x+1$" part means that there's some sort of shifting going on, but we can't see what it is.

We'll need some way to get this thing in our easy graphing form!

$$y = a(x-h)^2 + k$$

The amazing trickery that will get our desired result is called completing the square. It's not too bad, once you get used to it. But, first, I need to remind you what a "square" is -- actually, a perfect square. Remember when we were factoring (or solving) and we'd get something like this?

$$x^2 + 4x + 4 = (x+2)(x+2)$$

Well, just like we can write bb as b^2, we can write

$$(x+2)(x+2) = (x+2)^2$$

It's a square!

Here are some perfect square quadratics:

$$y = x^2 + 6x + 9 = (x+3)(x+3) = (x+3)^2$$
$$y = x^2 - 8x + 16 = (x-4)(x-4) = (x-4)^2$$
$$y = x^2 + 5x + \frac{25}{4} = (x+\frac{5}{2})(x+\frac{5}{2}) = (x+\frac{5}{2})^2$$

We'll be aiming for guys like these in our trick. Keep reading to see how it works.

Quadratics - Graphing by Completing the Square - How

Here we go!

Let's turn this guy: $y = x^2 + 10x - 3$

into the form: $y = a(x-h)^2 + k$

This is a trick -- it's just a few steps to go through ... and it will <u>always</u> work. This is one of the few times I will be telling you that this is just a process to memorize. It's a zero-thinking process. Go into robot mode! If you know how to do it, it's a snap -- a slam dunk. If you don't know how to do it, you have NO hope of getting it right. There's no way to guess your way through this one!

Let's do it!

$$y = x^2 + 10x - 3$$

<u>STEP 1</u>: Put a box around the last guy...

$$y = x^2 + 10x \,\boxed{-3}$$

and say out loud, "Do not touch the -3!"
(You'll thank me for this later.)

STEP 2: Put some ( ) and ___ in like this:

$$y = (x^2 + 10x \underline{\quad}) - 3 \underline{\quad}$$

STEP 3:

$$y = (x^2 + 10x \underline{\quad}) - 3 \underline{\quad}$$

Take half of this guy and put a circle around him:

$$\tfrac{1}{2}(10) = \enspace ⑤$$

STEP 4: Square circled guy...

$$y = (x^2 + 10x \underline{+25}) - 3 \underline{\quad}$$

$(5)^2 = 25$ and put it here

STEP 5: THIS IS THE MOST FORGOTTEN STEP!

Remember that equations are like see-saws... We have to keep them balanced!

We just plopped 25 pounds onto the right side of our equation:

$$y = (x^2 + 10x \underline{+25}) - 3 \underline{\quad}$$

So... we'll just take it back off!

$$y = (x^2 + 10x + \underline{25}) - 3 - \underline{25}$$

* That's why you had to put a blank at the end... So, you wouldn't forget this!

STEP 6: Finish it off:

$$y = (x^2 + 10x + 25) - 28$$

Go back and get circled guy.

$$y = (x+5)^2 - 28$$
↗
circled guy

We're all done and can now graph this guy.

$$y = (x+5)^2 - 28$$
↗   ↓ down 28
$x = -5$
← 5

We can always check our answers on these by multiplying them back out!

$$y = (x+5)^2 - 28 = (x+5)(x+5) - 28 \qquad \text{yep!}$$
↙
$$= x^2 + 10x + 25 - 28 = x^2 + 10x - 3$$

Let's do another one:

$$y = x^2 - 6x + 3$$

STEP 1:

$$y = x^2 - 6x \boxed{+3}$$

Do not touch the + 3!

STEP 2:

$$y = (x^2 - 6x \underline{\quad}) + 3 \underline{\quad}$$

STEP 3:

$$y = (x^2 - 6x \underline{\quad}) + 3 \underline{\quad}$$

$$\tfrac{1}{2}(-6) = \boxed{-3} \leftarrow \text{circled guy}$$

STEP 4:

$$y = (x^2 - 6x \underline{+9}) + 3 \underline{\quad}$$

$$(-3)^2 = 9$$

STEP 5:

$$y = (x^2 - 6x + 9) + 3 - 9$$

STEP 6:

$$y = (x-3)^2 - 6$$

circled guy

Check it:

_____

Your turn:

  Complete the square: $y = x^2 - 4x + 5$

_____

  Complete the square: $y = x^2 + 6x + 5$

Quadratics - Graphing by Completing the Square - Freaky Things That Can Happen

Completing the square is pretty easy when the coefficient on the x^2 is one...

When it isn't, things get a little sticky.

Let's do this guy:

$$y = 3x^2 + 12x + 11$$

STEP 1:   Like before...

$$y = 3x^2 + 12x \underline{\lfloor +11}$$

Do not touch the +11!

STEP 2:   Identify the trouble-maker:

Who's a problem?

$$y = 3x^2 + 12x \underline{\lfloor +11}$$

Pure trouble, Baby!

We CANNOT complete the square with this 3 here -- the x^2 must be alone!

So, we factor him out... of both x guys -- not the 11! You can't touch him.

$$y = 3(x^2 + 4x) \underline{\lfloor +11}$$

Now, we can go ahead with the rest of the process. Just don't forget about that 3 who's hanging around in the front.

STEP 3:

$$y = 3(x^2 + 4x \underline{\quad}) + 11 \underline{\quad}$$

STEP 4:

$$y = 3(x^2 + 4x \underline{\quad}) + 11 \underline{\quad}$$

$$\tfrac{1}{2}(4) = \boxed{2} \leftarrow \text{circled guy}$$

STEP 5:

$$y = 3(x^2 + 4x \underline{+4}) + 11 \underline{\quad}$$

$$(2)^2 = 4 \qquad \text{circled guy squared}$$

STEP 6: Remember to balance it out!
But, be careful ... IT'S A TRAP!

How much weight did we really add on?
4 pounds? NO!

$$y = 3(x^2 + 4x + 4) + 11 \underline{\quad}$$

$$+12$$

We really plunked on 12 pounds because the 3 distributes in to the 4!

So, take 12 pounds off on the end:

$$y = 3(\underbrace{x^2 + 4x + 4}_{+12}) + 11 \underline{-12}$$

STEP 7: Finish it off... Where's circled guy?

$$y = 3(x+2)^2 - 1$$
                    ↑
                circled guy

Done! He's ready to graph!

Do it:

_____

Let's walk through another one:

$$y = -2x^2 + 12x - 13$$

STEP 1:

$$y = -2x^2 + 12x \underline{|-13}$$
                        ↗
              Do not touch the −13!

STEP 2: Factor out the trouble-maker:

$$y = -2(x^2 - 6x) \underline{|-13}$$

Careful here! Watch your signs!
* Just distribute back through to check.

STEP 3:

$$y = -2(x^2 - 6x \underline{\quad}) + 13 \underline{\quad}$$

STEP 4:

$$y = -2(x^2 - 6x \underline{\quad}) + 13 \underline{\quad}$$

$$\tfrac{1}{2}(-6) = \boxed{-3} \leftarrow \text{circled guy}$$

STEP 5:

$$y = -2(x^2 - 6x \underline{+9}) - 13 \underline{\quad}$$

$$(-3)^2 = 9 \quad \text{circled guy squared}$$

STEP 6:

$$y = -2(x^2 - 6x + 9) - 13 \underline{+18}$$

$$-18 \qquad \text{undo it!}$$

STEP 7:

$$y = -2(x-3)^2 + 5$$

circled guy

Check it by multiplying it back out:

_____

Graph it:

_____

Your turn:

$$y = 2x^2 + 20x + 43$$

_____

$$y = -5x^2 - 20x - 17$$

Here's another creepy guy... He looks so easy, but students tend to mess him up.

$$y = -x^2 + 12x - 32$$

Just an innocent looking -1 in front...

We just have to be extra careful with the signs!

STEP 1:

$$y = -x^2 + 12x \boxed{-32}$$

Do not touch the -32!

STEP 2: Factor out the trouble-maker:

$$y = -(x^2 - 12x) \boxed{-32}$$

Watch this sign!

STEP 3:

$$y = -(x^2 - 12x \underline{\quad}) - 32 \underline{\quad}$$

STEP 4:

$$y = -(x^2 - 12x \underline{\quad}) - 32 \underline{\quad}$$

$$\tfrac{1}{2}(-12) = \boxed{-6} \leftarrow \text{circled guy}$$

STEP 5:

$$y = -(x^2 - 12x \underline{+36}) - 32 \underline{\quad}$$

$$(-6)^2 = 36$$

STEP 6:

$$y = -(x^2 - 12x + 36) - 32 \; \underline{+36}$$

-36

Careful!!

undo it!

STEP 7:

$$y = -(x-6)^2 + 4$$

↑ circled guy

Check it:

_____

Try it:

$$y = -x^2 - 6x - 11$$

ARE YOU
TOTALLY
STRESSED OUT?

You don't have to feel out of control. You don't have to feel nervous.
You don't have to feel tired and foggy all the time. Believe me, I've
been there myself. I totally remember what it was like to be a
student -- and I was a student for a LONG time! Since then, I've
been a college teacher so I'm around students all the time - most of
them stressed out. Over the years, I've been teaching my students
how to de-stress and how to deal with stress... I finally decided to
make a stress management site specially designed FOR students --
and anyone else who feels stressed out.

So, settle down and KNOW that you CAN lower your stress! You
really ARE in control of what's going on in your world!
YOU CAN ACTUALLY BE HAPPY AND RELAXED -- yeah, even
while you're a student!

TotallyStressedOut.com
The stress management site for students

Are you already in credit card trouble?
Is your FICO score the pits?
Uh... FICO who?
Do you want to learn about this stuff?

Do you want to learn how
to be SMART & RICH?

financeFREAK.com

A fool and his money are soon parted.
Don't be a fool... Be a FREAK!

COMPLEX NUMBERS

Complex Numbers - What are They?

So far, in your math career, you've been working with real numbers. (Even though some of your answers on math tests have been unreal. haha!)

All the guys that appear on the number line are real numbers (in the real number system):

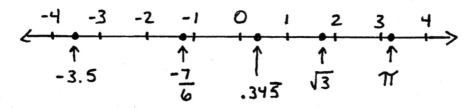

You've probably been told (even by me) that you couldn't do $\sqrt{-4}$ yet because of that negative sign. The reason is that the answer isn't a real number. Yes, there <u>is</u> an answer! (Try to calm down -- I know this is terribly exciting.) There is an answer... and it's imaginary. No, I'm not making this up.

Here it is:

$$\sqrt{4} = 2$$

$$\sqrt{-4} = 2i \leftarrow \text{That's an "i" for imaginary number.}$$

So, what's the i?

$$i = \sqrt{-1}$$

For the imaginary number system, we just define it this way:

$$i = \sqrt{-1}$$

With this, we can do a lot of cool things we couldn't do before. One of the coolest things in math (stop laughing -- there are some) is made with imaginary numbers:

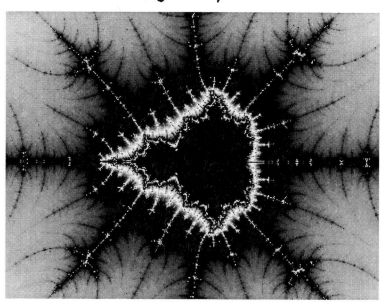

You should see them in full color. Pretty wild! For more info, check out

coolmath.com/fractals

OK, lets go back to $\sqrt{-4} = 2i$...

Here's what really happened with this problem:

$$\sqrt{-4} = \sqrt{(4)(-1)} = \sqrt{4}\sqrt{-1} = 2i$$

So...

$$\sqrt{-25} = 5i \qquad \sqrt{-49} = 7i \qquad \sqrt{-13} = \sqrt{13}\,i$$

We can't pop the $\sqrt{13}$, so we just pull the i out.

A complex number is made up of a real number and an imaginary number.

Here are a few:

$$3 + 2i \qquad -4 + 5i \qquad \frac{5}{2} - \frac{\sqrt{3}}{2}i$$

The official form is:

$$a + bi$$

the real part   the imaginary part

Complex Numbers - Factoring

Remember the difference of two squares?
We can factor this guy:

$$x^2 - 9 = (x-3)(x+3)$$

You've probably been told that you couldn't factor this guy...

$$x^2 + 9$$
$$\uparrow$$

The <u>sum</u> of two squares.

Well, they fibbed... You <u>can</u> factor this guy...
Just not with real numbers.

We just need one more thing though:

$$\text{Since } i = \sqrt{-1}$$

Squaring both side gives $\boxed{i^2 = -1}$

So, check this out:

I claim that

$$x^2 + 9 \text{ factors as } (x-3i)(x+3i)$$
$$\nearrow$$

Just like the difference of two squares... but with i's after the numbers.

Does it work? Let's check it using FOIL!

$$(x-3i)(x+3i) = x^2 + 3ix - 3ix - 9i^2$$

You treat the i guys just like regular variables... adding "like terms" etc.

And, we know that $i^2 = -1$...

$$(x-3i)(x+3i) = x^2 + 3ix - 3ix - 9i^2$$
$$= x^2 + 3ix - 3ix - 9(-1)$$
$$= x^2 + 9$$

Whoa, Dude... It worked!

$$x^2 + 9 = (x-3i)(x+3i)$$

Here's another one:

$$x^2 + 25 = (x-5i)(x+5i)$$

Try it:

$$x^2 + 36 =$$

$$9x^2 + 64 =$$

$$x^2 + 1 =$$

Complex Numbers - The Quadratic Formula

There's one main place that complex numbers will pop up on you:

The Quadratic Formula!

Sometimes, you'll get negative numbers under that radical.

Here's an example:

$$\text{Solve } x^2 - 6x + 25 = 0$$

$$x = \frac{6 \pm \sqrt{36 - 4(25)}}{2} = \frac{6 \pm \sqrt{-64}}{2} = \frac{6 \pm 8i}{2}$$

Which you can rewrite as

$$= \frac{6}{2} \pm \frac{8i}{2} = 3 \pm 4i$$

So, the solutions are $\boxed{3 - 4i \text{ and } 3 + 4i.}$

Here's another one:

$$\text{Solve } 2x^2 + x + 10 = 0$$

$$x = \frac{-1 \pm \sqrt{1 - 4(2)(10)}}{4} = \frac{-1 \pm \sqrt{-79}}{4} = \frac{-1 \pm \sqrt{79}\,i}{4}$$

$$\left\{ \frac{-1 - \sqrt{79}\,i}{4}, \frac{-1 + \sqrt{79}\,i}{4} \right\}$$

Your turn:

Solve $x^2 - 10x + 29$

_____

Solve $4x^2 - x + 7$

_____

Now, try solving this guy:

$$x^2 + 25 = 0$$

WAY 1: FACTOR

$x^2 + 25 = 0$

$(x - 5i)(x + 5i) = 0$

$x - 5i = 0$ or $x + 5i = 0$

$x = 5i$ $x = -5i$

$\{-5i, 5i\}$

WAY 2: SQUARE ROOT TRICK

$x^2 + 25 = 0$

$x^2 = -25$

$\sqrt{x^2} = \sqrt{-25}$

$x = \pm 5i$

$\{-5i, 5i\}$

Your turn... and do it both ways:

Solve $x^2 + 81 = 0$

Hey, have you noticed something interesting with all our answers?

$$\{ 3-4i, \ 3+4i \}$$

$$\left\{ \frac{-1}{4} - \frac{\sqrt{79}}{4}i, \ \frac{-1}{4} + \frac{\sqrt{79}}{4}i \right\}$$

$$\{ -5i, \ 5i \}$$

↑

Look at this last guy in his official complex number form:

$$\{ 0-5i, \ 0+5i \}$$

Each of these answers is a pair -- one with a minus and one with a plus. Like

$$\{ a-bi, \ a+bi \}$$

These are called complex conjugates.
For example, the conjugate of

$$-5 + 3i \quad \text{is} \quad -5 - 3i$$

↑ plus   ↑ minus

When you are solving quadratic equations, each complex solution will <u>always</u> have his conjugate buddy with him!

Are you already in credit card trouble?
Is your FICO score the pits?
Uh... FICO who?
Do you want to learn about this stuff?

Do you want to learn how
to be SMART & RICH?

financeFREAK.com

A fool and his money are soon parted.
Don't be a fool... Be a FREAK!

SYSTEMS
OF
EQUATIONS

Systems - 2x2's: Solving by Graphing

Systems, 2x2 in this case, are when you have 2 equations and 2 unknowns (letters).

Here's an example:

$$x + y = 3$$
$$x - 2y = 0$$

The goal is to find an x guy and a y guy that work in both equations.

In this chapter, I'll show you three different ways to solve these.

The first method is graphing. This is a cool method to start with since it lets you see what's going on.

We've got two equations -- and they are equations of lines. Let's graph them both on the same axes and see what we get.

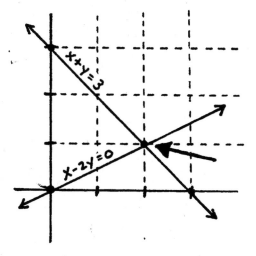

Hey, the two lines intersect at the point (2,1).

This means that (2,1) is a point in <u>both</u> lines...

So, x = 2 and y = 1 will work in the equations!

$$x + y = 3 \rightarrow 2 + 1 = 3 \text{ yep}$$
$$x - 2y = 0 \rightarrow 2 - 2(1) = 3 \text{ yep}$$

So, the answer is (2,1).

Checking your answers, like we did at the end there, is a really good idea... and something you should always do on a test! We're going to do it on every single problem we do!

Here's another one:

$$X + 2y = -2$$
$$3x - 2y = -6$$

Graph them!

Well, it <u>looks</u> like they intersect at (-2,0). But, what if it's really (-1.999, 0.001)? We have to check to be sure!

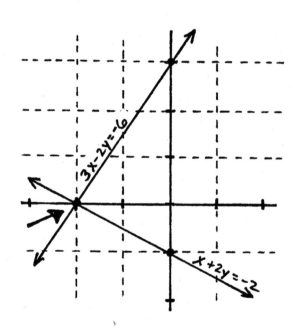

$$X + 2y = -2 \rightarrow -2 + 2(0) = -2$$
$$3x - 2y = -6 \rightarrow 3(-2) - 2(0) = -6$$

Yep! So, the answer is (-2,0).

Try it:

 Solve by graphing: $x - y = 5$
$3x + 2y = 0$

This is a cool method for getting you to see what's going on. But, it has serious problems. What if you get a graph like this?

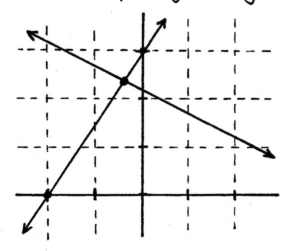

What's the answer?
Uh... $(-.4, 2.3)$?
$(-.41, 2.29)$?
There's no way to tell.

So, unless the problem is designed to cross at a nice, clean point, the graphing method is pretty useless for solving systems.

Let's start with a problem that's half done already... We already know what y is:

$$5x + 3y = 7$$
$$y = 4$$

We just need to figure out what the x is. Substitution! Take the y guy and stick it into the first equation:

$$5x + 3y = 7$$
$$y = \boxed{4}$$

This gives $5x + 3(4) = 7$ Solve for x!

$$5x + 12 = 7$$
$$\underline{-12 \quad -12}$$
$$5x = -5$$
$$\boxed{x = -1}$$

Let's double-check that: $5(-1) + 3(4) = 7$

So, the solution to our system is $\underline{(-1, 4)}$.

Remember that this is a point where two lines intersect.

Try it:

Solve by substitution: $2x + 5y = -4$
$$x = 3$$

Let's do another one where we get a bit of a head start:

$$3x - 7y = -14$$
$$x = 2y - 3$$

Notice that one equation is solved for x... Let's stick that x blob into the other equation in place of x:

$$3x - 7y = -14$$
$$x = \boxed{2y - 3}$$

This gives us

$$3(2y-3) - 7y = -14 \qquad \text{Solve for } y$$
$$6y - 9 - 7y = -14$$
$$-y - 9 = -14$$
$$\underline{ +9 \qquad +9}$$

$$-y = -5$$
$$\boxed{y = 5}$$

OK, we've got y... Now, we need x... See the circled blob on the previous page? Stick it in there! (That's why I circled it!)

$$x = \boxed{2y - 3}$$
$$y = \boxed{5}$$

$$x = 2(5) - 3 = 7$$
$$\boxed{x = 7}$$

Is our answer (7, 5)? Let's check... and you have to check it in **both** equations!

$$3x - 7y = -14 \quad \rightarrow \quad 3(7) - 7(5) = -14 \quad \text{yep}$$
$$x = 2y - 3 \qquad\qquad 7 = 2(5) - 3 \quad \text{yep}$$

So, the answer is (7, 5).

Try it:

Solve by substitution:
$$4x - 3y = 25$$
$$y = 6x - 13$$

OK, let's do one all the way from the beginning:

$$10x + y = 35$$
$$4x - 7y = -23$$

We've got to rewrite one of these equations so it's like

$$y = xstuff \quad or \quad x = ystuff$$

And here's the key to making your life happier:

> You don't want fractions!

If possible, you want to pick a guy to solve for that doesn't create fractions.

Check it out:

If we solve for this guy...   it's nice and clean!

$$10x + y = 35 \rightarrow y = \boxed{35 - 10x}$$
$$4x - 7y = -23$$

Circle it and stick it in the OTHER equation.

$$4x - 7(35 - 10x) = -23 \quad \text{Solve for } x$$
$$4x - 245 + 70x = -23$$
$$74x - 245 = -23$$
$$74x = 222$$
$$\boxed{x = 3} \quad \text{Whew! That was getting icky!}$$

Now, you stick this guy $x = ③$
into circled guy! $y = \boxed{35 - 10X}$

$y = 35 - 10(3)$

$\boxed{y = 5}$

I think we've got it... $(3, 5)$... <u>Check it!</u>

* in both equations!

Let's go back and look at the way we started that problem again:

$$10X + y = 35$$
$$4X - 7y = -23$$

What if we'd solved for this guy instead?

$$10X + y = 35$$
$$4X - 7y = -23 \rightarrow 4X = 7y - 23$$
$$x = \boxed{\frac{7}{4}y - \frac{23}{4}}$$

Yuck!

$$10\left(\frac{7}{4}y - \frac{23}{4}\right) + y = 35$$

Oh, please... Don't make me go on!

That thing got brutal fast!

So, if you can, always solve for a guy with no coefficient in front... Go for an x or -x or y or -y.

In my opinion, problems like this guy

$$3x + 8y = 2$$
$$2x - 7y = -11$$

Should be done with the method in the next section.

Your turn:

Solve by substitution: $5x + 8y = 11$
                          $x + 3y = -9$

Let's just do one and you'll see how it works:

$$2x + 3y = 20$$
$$-2x + y = 4$$
$$\uparrow$$

See how these guys are the same, but with a different sign?

If we add the two equations -- straight down, those x critters are going to drop right out! Just add "like terms" and drag the " = " down to:

$$2x + 3y = 20$$
$$+ \quad \underline{-2x + y = 4}$$
$$0 + 4y = 24$$
$$4y = 24$$
$$\boxed{y = 6}$$

We've got one of them... Now, we just need to get the x. To do this, you can stick the y into either of the original equations... The second equation is easier:

$$-2x + y = 4 \qquad y = \boxed{6}$$
$$-2x + 6 = 4$$
$$-2x = -2$$
$$\boxed{x = 1}$$

It looks like the answer is $(1, 6)$.
Check it! (In <u>both</u> equations!)

_____

Try it:

Solve by elimination: $7x + 4y = 2$
$9x - 4y = 30$

* Notice that the y
is ready to drop out!

_____

Most of the time they aren't set up that nicely.
You'll usually have to do a little dinking before
something will drop out.

Look at this one:

$$3x - 4y = -5$$
$$5x - 2y = -6$$

If we just add straight down, nothing's going
to drop out and we'll just get a mess.

But, check out the y guys:

$$3x - 4y = -5$$
$$5x - 2y = -6$$

If we could make this a +4y,
the y's would drop out...

So, let's do it! Remember that we can
multiply an equation by a number... So, let's
multiply the second equation by −2:

$$3x - 4y = -5$$
$$-2(5x - 2y = -6)$$

Remember to hit
each guy!

$$\rightarrow$$

$$3x - 4y = -5$$
$$-10x + 4y = 12 \quad +$$
$$\overline{-7x + 0 = 7}$$
$$-7x = 7$$
$$\boxed{x = -1}$$

Now, stick the x guy into either of the original
equations. I'm going to go for the first one:

$$x = \boxed{-1}$$

$$3x - 4y = -5$$
$$3(-1) - 4y = -5$$
$$-3 - 4y = -5$$
$$-4y = -2$$
$$\boxed{y = \tfrac{1}{2}}$$

The answer is $(-1, \frac{1}{2})$.

Check it — and don't let that fraction freak you... These things happen!

Your turn:

Solve by elimination:

$$2x + 5y = 5$$
$$-6x + 7y = -37$$

*Hint: ditch the x!

Sometimes, you'll have to make adjustments to both equations to get something to drop out. When possible, always go after the easier numbers!

Let's do this one:

$$2x - 9y = 8$$
$$-5x + 8y = -20$$

↑ These numbers are easier than the -9 and 8.

We want to make these $10x$ and $-10x$:

$$5(2x - 9y = 8)$$
$$2(-5x + 8y = -20)$$

$\rightarrow$

$$10x - 45y = 40$$
$$-10x + 16y = -40$$
$$\overline{-29y = 0}$$
$$\boxed{y = 0}$$

Remember to hit each guy! It's easy to forget the last guys.

Let's stick $y = 0$ into the first equation:

$$y = \boxed{0}$$

$$2x - 9\overset{\curvearrowleft}{y} = 8$$
$$2x - 9(0) = 8$$
$$2x = 8$$
$$\boxed{x = 4}$$

The answer is $(4, 0)$.

Check it!

Your turn:

Solve by elimination: $13x - 2y = 25$
$4x + 3y = -14$

*Use your head...
Which numbers are easier?

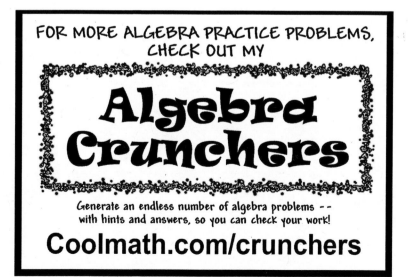

Remember that a typical solution to a system is a point like $(-2, 3)$ where the two lines intersect.

But, sometimes this doesn't happen!

Graph these two lines:

$$x + y = 1$$
$$x + y = 4$$

What's the solution? They have to intersect to get a solution. But, that's never going to happen since these lines are parallel. So, there is no (x, y) that is going to work in both equations.

When you are solving by elimination or substitution, you'll be going about your work... without a care in the world... and something freaky is going to happen! You're going to get a false statement like

$$0 = 8$$

Something like this is sure to produce a sick stomach during a test! But, not to worry. You won't panic, because you'll know what this means. It just means that the two lines don't intersect. For the official answer, you'll want to write something like this:

> These lines are parallel.
> There is no solution.

Try it:

Solve by either elimination or substitution. Then, check your answer by graphing:

$$3x - y = 6$$
$$6x - 2y = 3$$

The other freaky thing that can happen is that the two lines can be lying right on top of each other -- they are the same line.

Graph these two lines:

$$x + y = 3$$
$$-2x - 2y = -6$$

So, what the heck does this mean for our answer? Every single (x,y) point that appears in one line appears in the other. So, every x and y combination that works in one equation, works in the other equation. And how many points are in a line? That's right, baby, there's an infinite number of them! So, how many points that work in one line work in the other? An infinite number. You should write something like this for your answer:

These are the same line, so there are an infinite number of solutions.

How is this little critter going to announce itself to you?

When you're solving by elimination or substitution... You'll be going along... and you'll get this:

$$0 = 0$$

A true statement, but not very helpful unless you know what you're doing -- and you do!

Try it:

Solve by either elimination or substitution. Then, check your answer by graphing:

$$x - y = -2$$
$$-3x + 3y = 6$$

Systems - 2x2's: Inequalities

First, let's do a quick review of graphing line inequalities:

Let's graph

$$x + y \leq 3$$

Graphing the line, itself, should be a no-brainer for you... But, figuring out which side should be shading is often the snag.

Here's the line:

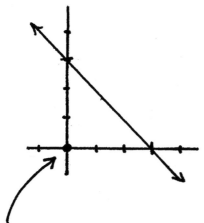

The line is solid because of the "$=$" in the $\leq$...

So... what side gets shaded?

To figure this out, we just pick a point that is <u>not</u> on the line and see if it works in

$$x + y \leq 3.$$

Let's try $(0,0)$ since it's so easy to work with:

$$x + y \leq 3$$
$$0 + 0 \leq 3 \quad \leftarrow \text{ Is this true?}$$
$$\text{Yep!}$$

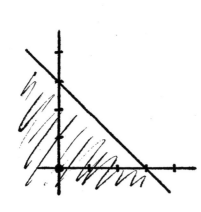

If $(0,0)$ works, then everything on his side of the line will work -- so, shade that side! If it didn't work, then we'd shade the other.

Your turn:

Graph $y \geq 2x-3$

Let's try another one:

$$y > \tfrac{1}{2}x$$

Remember how to graph $y = \tfrac{1}{2}x$? Think $y = mx+b$!

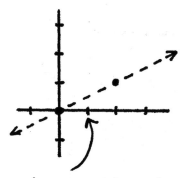

The line is dashed since there is no "=" in the $>$.
What side do we shade?
Pick a point <u>not</u> on the line and try it!

Let's try $(1,0)$...

$$y > \tfrac{1}{2}x$$
$$0 > \tfrac{1}{2}(1)$$

Nope! This doesn't work!
So, shade the other side.

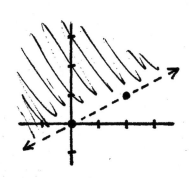

Remember, that this means that all the points in the shaded area work in our inequality

$$y > \tfrac{1}{2}x.$$

Try it:

Graph $x > \tfrac{1}{3}y$ (Be careful! Get it in $y=mx+b$ form!)

OK, now let's do a system:

$$x + y \leq 3$$

$$x > -1$$

We just graph each one and see where they overlap.

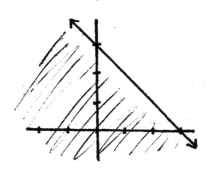 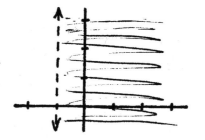

What will the intersection look like?

Knowing what this point is is going to be really important in the next section!

It looks like it's (-1,4), but we need to be sure. Remember that the point of intersection is the solution to the system

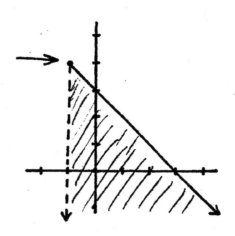

$$x + y = 3$$
$$x = -1$$

We have the x guy, so stick him into the other equation:

$$x + y = 3$$
$$-1 + y = 3$$
$$y = 4$$

Yep, the point is (-1,4), so here's our official answer:

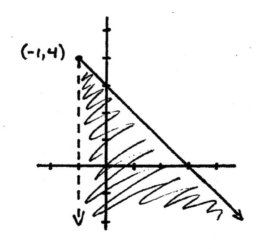

(-1,4)

Your turn:

Graph $x + y < 4$

$\qquad x - y \geq -2$

Here's one that's more complicated:

$x + y \leq 8$ Sure, it looks like a lot... But,
$y \leq x + 4$ just take each line one at a
$x \leq 5$ time!
$\left.\begin{array}{l} x \geq 0 \\ y \geq 0 \end{array}\right\}$ ← This combo means that we are
        in the first quadrant:

So, we just need to concentrate on that...

Here's the shaded area:

　*　You should graph all this on your own on a separate piece of paper for the practice!

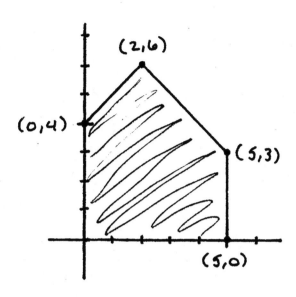

All the points of intersection need to be checked:

(0,4) should be where	(2,6) should be where
$y = x + 4$ $x = 0$ intersect... Does the point work?	$y = x + 4$ $x + y = 8$ intersect... Does the point work?
(5,3) should be where $x + y = 8$ $x = 5$ intersect... Does the point work?	(5,0) should be where $x = 5$ $y = 0$ intersect... This one obviously works!

Your turn:

Graph and identify (and double check) all points of intersection:

$$-x + y \leq 2$$
$$x + y \leq 6$$
$$y \leq 3$$
$$y \geq 0$$
$$x \geq 0$$

Systems - 3x3's: A Brief Intro

Before, we learned how to solve systems with two equations and two unknowns... 2x2's.

Here's an example of the type we solved:

$$x + y = 3$$
$$x - 2y = 0$$

Remember that these are two lines:

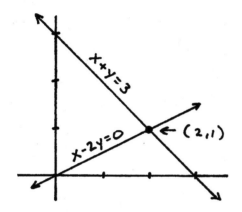

The point where the two lines intersect is the solution:

$$(2, 1)$$

So, $x = 2$ and $y = 1$ work in <u>BOTH</u> equations.

Now, we're going to do 3x3's -- systems with three equations and three unknowns.
Like this guy:

$$x - y + z = 7$$
$$2x + 3y - z = -8$$
$$4x + y - 2z = -6$$

So, what the heck is something like

$$x - y + z = 7?$$

Well, when we have two variables, x and y, we have a line... and we graph them on a

2-dimensional plane. So, with three variables, x, y and z, we'll be in three dimensions... That's 3-D space!

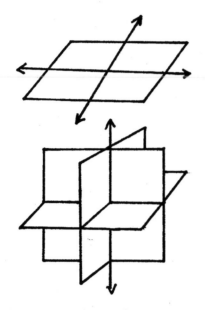

Pretend that the floor of the room you are in is our old x-y plane...

The third dimension will be the vertical line shooting up from the corner of the room.

This is really all you need to worry about... unless you're going to take Calculus 3. (Which is a very cool class, by the way! Cough-geek!)

So, an equation like

$$x - y + z = 7$$

is a plane that lives in 3-D space.

With a system of three equations and three unknowns, we've got three planes in 3-D space.

Look in the corner of your room again... That little corner is the one point where the two walls and the floor (or the ceiling -- depending on where you're looking) intersect.

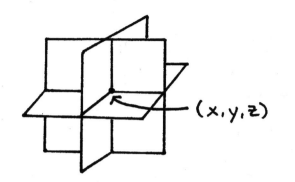

(x,y,z)

So, hopefully, we'll get a nice (x,y,z) point like (1,-2,4) for an answer. (check out the "Freaky Things" lesson!)

This means that $x=1$, $y=-2$, $z=4$ will work in ALL three of the original equations you started with.

After you're done solving a system, you'll be able to check your answers.

Check it out:

By magic, we know that (1,-2,4) is the solution to the system

$$x - y + z = 7$$
$$2x + 3y - z = -8$$
$$4x + y - 2z = -6$$

Let's check that!

$x - y + z = 7$
$1 - (-2) + 4 = 7$
$7 = 7$
yep!

$2x + 3y - z = -8$
$2(1) + 3(-2) - 4 = -8$
$-8 = -8$
yep!

$4x + y - 2z = -6$
$4(1) + (-2) - 2(4) = -6$
$-6 = -6$
yep!

It's <u>really</u> important to check all three equations. It's possible to make a mistake and have your answers work in one or two of them!

Try it:

Verify that $(5, -1, 2)$ is the solution to

$$5x - 2y + z = 29$$
$$-3x + 4y - 2z = -23$$
$$x + 6y - 7z = -15$$

Solving 3x3 systems of equations works a lot like the 2x2 method of elimination -- with a little substitution mixed in. It really isn't hard, but it takes good organization skills. The problems are a bit long, but I'll show you how to work through them and how to keep things organized.

Instead of starting out by working through an entire problem (which would look pretty creepy), let's start with some that are almost finished already.

Remember that our goal is to find the values for x, y and z. (or whatever letters you have.)

Let's finish solving this guy... As you can see, we already know what z is!

$$2x - y + 6z = 20$$
$$5y - 3z = -2$$
$$z = 4$$

What we're going to do is called "back substitution" because we're going to work our way back up through the equations, starting at the bottom with that z.

Take the value for z and stick it into the equation with two variables... This will pop the y!

$$2x - y + 6z = 20$$
$$5y - 3z = -2$$
$$z = \boxed{4}$$

$$5y - 3(4) = -2$$
$$5y - 12 = -2$$
$$5y = 10$$
$$\boxed{y = 2}$$

Now, we have $z = 4$ and $y = 2$... Stick them both into the top equation and we'll get x!

$$2x - y + 6z = 20$$
$$2x - 2 + 6(4) = 20$$
$$2x - 2 + 24 = 20$$
$$2x + 22 = 20$$
$$2x = -2$$
$$\boxed{x = -1}$$

So, $x = -1$, $y = 2$ and $z = 4$. Since this is a point in space, we write the answer as a 3-D coordinate: $(-1, 2, 4)$

Yeah, that was just the <u>end</u> of one of these problems! Really, it just looks like a lot because of all my explaining.

Try it -- Just work your way back up:

$$x + 4y - 5z = 39$$
$$7y + 2z = 11$$
$$y = 3$$

This one will be a little less finished...

$$5x - 2y + z = -3$$
$$7y - 3z = -4$$
$$4y + 3z = 26$$

Notice that we have a nice little 2x2 system that will give us the y and z answers... Then, we'll just stick those into the first equation and we'll have x!

$$5x - 2y + z = -3$$
$$7y - 3z = -4$$
$$4y + 3z = 26$$

Working the 2x2, eliminate the z... to get y... Then, use the y to pop the z...

$$7y - 3z = -4$$
$$+ \ 4y + 3z = 26$$
$$\overline{11y = 22}$$
$$\boxed{y = 2}$$

$$7y - 3z = -4$$
$$7(2) - 3z = -4$$
$$14 - 3z = -4$$
$$-3z = -18$$
$$\boxed{z = 6}$$

Now, stick $y = 2$ and $z = 6$ into the first equation to pop x:

$$5x - 2y + z = -3$$
$$5x - 2(2) + 6 = -3$$
$$5x + 2 = -3$$
$$5x = -5$$
$$\boxed{x = -1}$$

So, the answer is $(-1, 2, 6)$.

Your turn:

$$5x - 3y + 9z = -47$$
$$2x + 7y = 13$$
$$4x + 5y = -1$$

Notice that the 2x2 is x and y this time. You'll pop z in the last step.

OK, let's start one from scratch:

$$2x - y + 5z = 4$$
$$x + y + z = -1$$
$$-3x + 2y - 6z = -7$$

The plan of attack is that we will use elimination to get rid of one variable ... We <u>must</u> use <u>all</u> three equations in this process! One of the most common mistakes is to try to solve a 3×3 using only two equations... You end up getting an answer that works in two of the equations and not in the third... which can really trick you on a test!

OK, first, let's get organized! Label the equations so you can keep track of your work (and so can your teacher!)

① $2x - y + 5z = 4$
② $x + y + z = -1$
③ $-3x + 2y - 6z = -7$

For this system, the y looks like the easiest one to get rid of ... So, let's ditch the y:

<u>STEP 1</u>: Use ① and ② to ditch the y:

① $2x - y + 5z = 4$ $2x - y + 5z = 4$
② $x + y + z = -1$ → $+ \underline{\; x + y + z = -1\;}$

put a box around it → $\boxed{3x + 6z = 3}$

STEP 2: Use ① and ③ to ditch the y:

① $(2x - y + 5z = 4)(2)$ $\longrightarrow$ $4x - 2y + 10z = 8$
③ $-3x + 2y - 6z = -7$ $+$ $\underline{-3x + 2y - 6z = -7}$
$$\boxed{x + 4z = 1}$$

Now, look at the two boxed guys... Those are our 2x2's! These will give us the values for x and z...

STEP 3: Solve the 2x2 ... ditch the x:

$3x + 6z = 3$ $\longrightarrow$ $3x + 6z = 3$
$-3(x + 4z = 1)$ $+$ $\underline{-3x - 12z = -3}$
$$-6z = 0$$

Circle him since it's one $\longrightarrow$ $\boxed{z = 0}$
of our answers!

Now substitute z = 0 into one of the 2x2 guys to get x:

$$x + 4z = 1$$
$$x + 4(0) = 1$$
$$\boxed{x = 1}$$

Now we finish it off by putting x = 1 and z = 0 into one of the original equations... Whichever one looks easy:

STEP 4: Pop the last guy!

② $x + y + z = -1$

$$1 + y + 0 = -1$$
$$y + 1 = -1$$
$$\boxed{y = -2}$$

So, the answer is $(1, -2, 0)$.
Whew!

Here's one more:

$$x + 2y - 5z = -11$$
$$4x - 3y + 2z = 11$$
$$-3x + 5y + 3z = 8$$

Always look for the path of least resistance...
The x looks like it's the easiest to get rid of!
Label the equations:

① $x + 2y - 5z = -11$

② $4x - 3y + 2z = 11$

③ $-3x + 5y + 3z = 8$

STEP 1: Use ① and ② to ditch the x:

① $(x + 2y - 5z = -11)(-4)$ $\quad -4x - 8y + 20z = 44$

② $4x - 3y + 2z = 11$ $\quad \rightarrow \quad + \underline{4x - 3y + 2z = 11}$

$$\boxed{-11y + 22z = 55}$$

STEP 2: Use ① and ③ to ditch the x:

① $(x + 2y - 5z = -11)(3)$ $\longrightarrow$ $3x + 6y - 15z = -33$
③ $-3x + 5y + 3z = 8$ $+ \underline{-3x + 5y + 3z = 8}$

$$\boxed{11y - 12z = -25}$$

STEP 3: Do the 2x2... ditch the y:

$-11y + 22z = 55$
$\underline{11y - 12z = -25}$
$10z = 30$

$\boxed{z = 3}$

$\longrightarrow$ $-11y + 22(3) = 55$
$-11y + 66 = 55$
$-11y = -11$

$\boxed{y = 1}$

STEP 4: Put $z = 3$ and $y = 1$ into one of the original equations:

① $x + 2y - 5z = -11$
$x + 2(1) - 5(3) = -11$
$x + 2 - 15 = -11$
$x - 13 = -11$

$\boxed{x = 2}$

The answer is $(2, 1, 3)$.

Remember that we can check our answer by putting it into **all** of the original equations:

① $x + 2y - 5z = -11$ $2 + 2(1) - 5(3) = -11$

② $4x - 3y + 2z = 11$ → $4(2) - 3(1) + 2(3) = 11$

③ $-3x + 5y + 3z = 8$ $-3(2) + 5(1) + 3(3) = 8$

All three work!

Your turn:

Do the first problem, but start by ditching the x... You'd better get the same answer I did!

$$2x - y + 5z = 4$$
$$x + y + z = -1$$
$$-3x + 2y - 6z = -7$$

Now, do the problem again, but start by ditching the z:

$$2x - y + 5z = 4$$
$$x + y + z = -1$$
$$-3x + 2y - 6z = -7$$

$$3x - 2y + 5z = 16$$
$$2x - y - 3z = 10$$
$$4x + 2y + 7z = 12$$

* Remember to ditch the easiest guy!

3x3's: Solving by Elimination

Systems - 3x3's: Freaky Things

Remember that a 3x3 system is really three planes that are living in 3-D space... They're actually locked into specific locations (not floating around) and we want to find where they intersect.

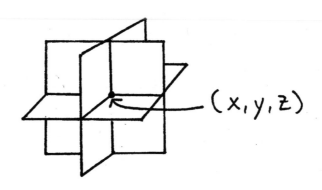

$$-(x, y, z)$$

But, the three planes might not all intersect in a nice little point.

Two of the planes might be parallel.

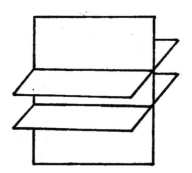

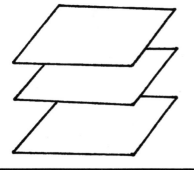

All three planes might be parallel.

or this could happen!

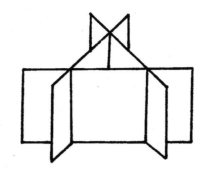

In all of the cases, you won't get a single point where all three planes intersect... So, there will be no solution.

When you are doing your elimination method, you'll be happily going along...
And you'll add two equations together and get a false statement like

$$0 = 4$$

When this happens, you'll know that there is no solution. For your answer, write something like

> " All three plane do not
> intersect in a single point.
> So, there is no solution."

The last freaky thing that can happen is that all three planes intersect in a line...

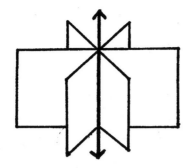

So, there are a ton of points along that line that work in all three equations. An infinite number!

When you are doing the elimination method, you'll be working through... adding those equations together... and BOOM! You'll get this:

$$0 = 0$$

Yeah, it's a true statement...
But, not very helpful.

When this happens, you'll know that the planes all intersect in a line -- and that line _is_ the answer! In some harder classes, you'll be shown how to find the equation of that line. For now, write something like this:

" The three planes intersect in a line. So, there are an infinite number of solutions."

Systems - 2x2's: Determinants and Cramer's Rule

You may or may not have seen this before -- it depends on where you took your last Algebra class.

First, I need to tell you about determinants. We'll be using these to solve systems.

Say you've got a 2x2:

$$x - 3y = 4$$
$$5x + 7y = 8$$

We can make something called a "coefficient matrix":

$$\begin{bmatrix} 1 & -3 \\ 5 & 7 \end{bmatrix}$$

A matrix is just a grid of numbers with brackets around them. (Remember that a coefficient is the number in front of the variable... $x = 1x$, so the coefficient is 1.) (We'll learn more about these matrix things in the next chapter.)

We've got rows and columns of the matrix:

$$\begin{bmatrix} 1 & -3 \\ 5 & 7 \end{bmatrix} \begin{matrix} \leftarrow \text{row 1} \\ \leftarrow \text{row 2} \end{matrix}$$

$\uparrow$ column 1 $\uparrow$ column 2

A determinant (which uses vertical lines instead of brackets)

$$\begin{vmatrix} 1 & -3 \\ 5 & 7 \end{vmatrix}$$

will give us a number that goes along with the matrix. We'll be able to use these numbers to solve systems! Woo hoo!

OK, so here's how you get the determinant -- it's really easy:

$$\begin{vmatrix} 1 & -3 \\ 5 & 7 \end{vmatrix} = (1)(7) - (5)(-3) = 22$$

Here's what I did:
I multiplied down this diagonal...

$$\begin{vmatrix} 1 & -3 \\ 5 & 7 \end{vmatrix} = (1)(7)$$

$$\begin{vmatrix} 1 & -3 \\ 5 & 7 \end{vmatrix} = (1)(7) - \quad \leftarrow \text{put a minus...}$$

then multiplied up this diagonal...

$$\begin{vmatrix} 1 & -3 \\ 5 & 7 \end{vmatrix} = (1)(7) - (5)(-3) = 22$$

Here's the general formula:

$$\begin{vmatrix} a & b \\ c & d \end{vmatrix} = ad - cb$$

Try it:

$$\begin{vmatrix} -2 & -6 \\ 5 & 8 \end{vmatrix} =$$

$$\begin{vmatrix} 3 & 9 \\ 2 & 6 \end{vmatrix}$$

Cramer's Rule uses determinants to solve systems and was named after the wacky guy on Seinfeld. (ok, I made that last part up.)

Let's just do one and I'll show you how it works:

$$3x - y = 7$$
$$-5x + 4y = -2$$

First, we'll get the determinant of the coefficient matrix -- we'll call it D:

$$D = \begin{vmatrix} 3 & -1 \\ -5 & 4 \end{vmatrix} = (3)(4) - (-5)(-1) = 7$$

Now, we're going to find two more determinants.

The first one we'll call D_x -- here's how it goes:

Take D...

$$\begin{vmatrix} 3 & -1 \\ -5 & 4 \end{vmatrix}$$ and delete the column for the x guys... $$\begin{vmatrix} & -1 \\ & 4 \end{vmatrix}$$ ↙ x guys ↙ y guys

Replace that column with the "= guys" (the 7 and the -2) and you get

$$D_x = \begin{vmatrix} 7 & -1 \\ -2 & 4 \end{vmatrix} = (7)(4) - (-2)(-1) = 26$$

To get the x part of our (x,y) solution, we take

$$x = \frac{D_x}{D} = \frac{26}{7}$$

Now, to get the y part...

Take D again...

$$\begin{vmatrix} 3 & -1 \\ -5 & 4 \end{vmatrix}$$ and delete the column for the y guys... $$\begin{vmatrix} 3 & \\ -5 & \end{vmatrix}$$ ↙ x guys ↙ y guys

Replace that column with the "= guys":

$$D_y = \begin{vmatrix} 3 & 7 \\ -5 & -2 \end{vmatrix} = (3)(-2) - (-5)(7) = 29$$

So, our y part is

$$y = \frac{D_y}{D} = \frac{29}{7}$$

and our final answer is $\left(\frac{26}{7}, \frac{29}{7} \right)$. That's it!

Your turn:

Use Cramer's Rule to solve

$$-6x + 8y = 17$$
$$13x - 2y = -4$$

I really think that Cramer's Rule is the easiest method for solving 2x2's. Especially if the answer is messy fractions (and it usually is)!

There's one little glitch...

Check this guy out:

$$7x - 7y = 8$$
$$-3x + 3y = 2$$

$$D = \begin{vmatrix} 7 & -7 \\ -3 & 3 \end{vmatrix} = (7)(3) - (-3)(-7) = 0$$

Whatever Dx and Dy are, we'll be stuck with this:

$$x = \frac{Dx}{0} \quad \text{and} \quad y = \frac{Dy}{0}$$

Zeros in denominators are bad news!

What does this mean? Well, we aren't going to get a nice (x,y) answer... In fact, we won't get any (x,y) answer! Either the lines are parallel or they are the same line. The only problem is that we can't tell. This is when you'll want to fall back on elimination to see which it is.

Which is it?

This is a trick that <u>ONLY</u> works for 3x3's. You cannot use it for 4x4's and higher... For these, the formal approach is a gnarly thing that expands around a row or column and uses critters called "minors." However, I highly recommend a computer or graphing calculator. If you go on to take Calculus 3 or Linear Algebra, you'll need the "real" 3x3 technique, but it will be specialized and really easy to pick up.

On to the trick...

It works a lot like the 2x2 method where you

$$\begin{vmatrix} a & b \\ c & d \end{vmatrix}$$

multiply down and add...

and multiply up and subtract.

$$\begin{vmatrix} a & b \\ c & d \end{vmatrix} \quad \begin{vmatrix} a & b \\ c & d \end{vmatrix} \rightarrow ad - cb$$

Here's the key:

$$\begin{vmatrix} a & b & c \\ d & e & f \\ g & h & i \end{vmatrix}\begin{matrix} a & b \\ d & e \\ g & h \end{matrix}$$

Copy the first two columns on the outside... and be neat about it!

Now, you'll multiply down and add...

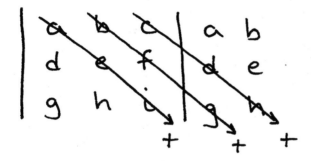

= aei + bfg + cdh...

Then, multiply up and subtract...

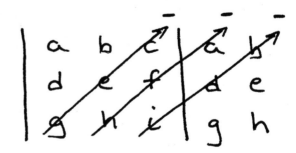

= aei + bfg + cdh - gec - hfa - idb

No, you don't have to memorize all these letters... Just learn the process!

Let's do one:

$$\begin{vmatrix} 1 & 2 & 3 \\ 4 & 5 & 6 \\ 7 & 8 & 9 \end{vmatrix}$$

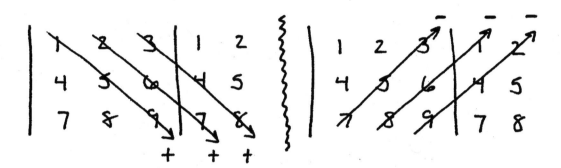

$$= (1)(5)(9) + (2)(6)(7) + (3)(4)(8)$$
$$- (7)(5)(3) - (8)(6)(1) - (9)(4)(2)$$

$$= 45 + 84 + 96 - 105 - 48 - 72 = 0$$

Here's another one... We just need to be careful with the negatives, so write out all your work really neatly!

$$\begin{vmatrix} 6 & -2 & 3 \\ -5 & 4 & 0 \\ -7 & 8 & 1 \end{vmatrix}$$

$$\begin{vmatrix} 6 & -2 & 3 \\ -5 & 4 & 0 \\ -7 & 8 & 1 \end{vmatrix} \begin{matrix} 6 & -2 \\ -5 & 4 \\ -7 & 8 \end{matrix} \quad \begin{matrix} 6 & -2 & 3 \\ -5 & 4 & 0 \\ -7 & 8 & 1 \end{matrix} \begin{matrix} 6 & -2 \\ -5 & 4 \\ -7 & 8 \end{matrix}$$

$$= (6)(4)(1) + (-2)(0)(-7) + (3)(-5)(8)$$
$$- (-7)(4)(3) - (8)(0)(6) - (1)(-5)(-2)$$

$$= 24 + 0 - 120 + 84 - 0 - 10 = -22$$

Your turn... and I'll give you a big hint:

The answer should be -348!

$$\begin{vmatrix} -2 & 8 & 6 \\ 4 & 1 & 0 \\ -5 & -3 & 9 \end{vmatrix}$$

Determinants for 3x3's are a little messier than they are for 2x2's. The determinants for 2x2's were a snap to crunch, so what we'll do is break down our big 3x3 guys into easy 2x2 critters.

Let's just jump right in and do one:

$$\begin{vmatrix} -2 & -9 & 4 \\ 3 & 7 & -5 \\ 1 & -6 & 8 \end{vmatrix}$$

Here's what you do:

Grab the row or column with the easiest numbers in it... Column 1 looks easy.

$$\begin{vmatrix} \boxed{-2} & -9 & 4 \\ 3 & 7 & -5 \\ 1 & -6 & 8 \end{vmatrix}$$

What we're going to do is called "expanding about the first column."

Before we start, we need a grid of +'s and −'s... Always start with a + in the upper left corner and go every other one:

$$\begin{vmatrix} + & - & + \\ - & + & - \\ + & - & + \end{vmatrix}$$

I'll call this our "sign box."

These are the ones that go along with our column. $\rightarrow$

$$\begin{vmatrix} \boxed{\begin{matrix} + \\ - \\ + \end{matrix}} & \begin{matrix} - \\ + \\ - \end{matrix} & \begin{matrix} + \\ - \\ + \end{matrix} \end{vmatrix}$$

Here we go:

Start with the first guy in our column...

$$\begin{vmatrix} \textcircled{-2} & -9 & 4 \\ 3 & 7 & -5 \\ 1 & -6 & 8 \end{vmatrix} = +(-2)$$

from the sign box

Block out the row and column that the -2 is in:

$$\begin{vmatrix} \textcircled{-2} & \cancel{-9} & \cancel{4} \\ 3 & 7 & -5 \\ 1 & -6 & 8 \end{vmatrix} = +(-2)\begin{vmatrix} 7 & -5 \\ -6 & 8 \end{vmatrix}$$

and take the determinant of what is left.

Now, go to the second guy in our column and do the same thing:

$$\begin{vmatrix} -2 & -9 & 4 \\ \textcircled{3} & \cancel{7} & \cancel{-5} \\ 1 & -6 & 8 \end{vmatrix} = +(-2)\begin{vmatrix} 7 & -5 \\ -6 & 8 \end{vmatrix} - (3)\begin{vmatrix} -9 & 4 \\ -6 & 8 \end{vmatrix}$$

from the sign box

Now do the last guy in the column:

$$\begin{vmatrix} -2 & -9 & 4 \\ 3 & 7 & -5 \\ 1 & -6 & 8 \end{vmatrix}$$

$$= +(-2)\begin{vmatrix} 7 & -5 \\ -6 & 8 \end{vmatrix} - (3)\begin{vmatrix} -9 & 4 \\ -6 & 8 \end{vmatrix} + (1)\begin{vmatrix} -9 & 4 \\ 7 & -5 \end{vmatrix}$$

Now, just pop the determinants and clean it up!

$$= -2\left[(7)(8)-(-6)(-5)\right] - 3\left[(-9)(8)-(-6)(4)\right]$$
$$+ 1\left[(-9)(-5)-(7)(4)\right]$$

Be careful! It's easy to make little boo-boos!

$$= -2(56-30) - 3(-72+24) + (45-28)$$
$$= -2(26) - 3(-48) + 17 = 109 \quad \text{Whew!}$$

This is always a bit overwhelming at first, so let's do another one:

$$\begin{vmatrix} -3 & 4 & 6 \\ 2 & 0 & -1 \\ 8 & -2 & 7 \end{vmatrix}$$ ← This row will be the easiest since it has a zero!

Here are our sign box guys. → $$\begin{vmatrix} + & - & + \\ - & + & - \\ + & - & + \end{vmatrix}$$

Here we go!

$$\begin{vmatrix} -3 & 4 & 6 \\ 2 & 0 & -1 \\ 8 & -2 & 7 \end{vmatrix}$$

We can ignore this chunk because of the zero!

$$= -(2)\begin{vmatrix} 4 & 6 \\ -2 & 7 \end{vmatrix} + 0\begin{vmatrix} \text{who} \\ \text{cares?} \end{vmatrix} - (-1)\begin{vmatrix} -3 & 4 \\ 8 & -2 \end{vmatrix}$$

$$= -2\left[(4)(7) - (-2)(6)\right] + 1\left[(-3)(-2) - (8)(4)\right]$$

$$= -2(28 + 12) + (6 - 32) = -2(40) - 26 = -106$$

Your turn!

$$\begin{vmatrix} 5 & -6 & 2 \\ 8 & -2 & 3 \\ 10 & 3 & 0 \end{vmatrix}$$

Systems - 3x3's: Cramer's Rule

Cramer's Rule for 3x3's works, pretty much, the same way it does for 2x2's -- it's the same pattern.

Let's solve this one:

$$2x - y + 6z = 10$$
$$-3x + 4y - 5z = 11$$
$$8x - 7y - 9z = 12$$

First, find the determinant of the coefficient matrix:

(I'm just going to crunch the determinants without showing the work -- you should check them!)

$$D = \begin{vmatrix} 2 & -1 & 6 \\ -3 & 4 & -5 \\ 8 & -7 & -9 \end{vmatrix} = -141$$

For a 3x3, we have 3 more determinants to find: D_x, D_y and D_z... Then we'll have

$$x = \frac{D_x}{D} \quad \text{and} \quad y = \frac{D_y}{D} \quad \text{and} \quad z = \frac{D_z}{D}$$

For D_x:

$$\begin{vmatrix} 2 & -1 & 6 \\ -3 & 4 & -5 \\ 8 & -7 & -9 \end{vmatrix}$$

and delete the column with the x guys...

↙ x guys

$$\begin{vmatrix} -1 & 6 \\ 4 & -5 \\ -7 & -9 \end{vmatrix}$$

Replace that column with the "= guys" and start crunching!

$$D_x = \begin{vmatrix} 10 & -1 & 6 \\ 11 & 4 & -5 \\ 12 & -7 & -9 \end{vmatrix} = -1499$$

So, $X = \dfrac{D_x}{D} = \dfrac{-1499}{-141} = \dfrac{1499}{141}$

For D_y:

Do the same kind of thing...

Take D again...

$$\begin{vmatrix} 2 & -1 & 6 \\ -3 & 4 & -5 \\ 8 & -7 & -9 \end{vmatrix} \quad \text{and delete the column with the y guys...} \quad \begin{vmatrix} 2 & & 6 \\ -3 & & -5 \\ 8 & & -9 \end{vmatrix} \leftarrow \text{y guys}$$

Replace that column with the "= guys" and crunch!

$$D_y = \begin{vmatrix} 2 & 10 & 6 \\ -3 & 11 & -5 \\ 8 & 12 & -9 \end{vmatrix} = -1492$$

So, $y = \dfrac{D_y}{D} = \dfrac{-1492}{-141} = \dfrac{1492}{141}$

Finally, for D_z:

You know how this is going to work...

Take D...

$$\begin{vmatrix} 2 & -1 & 6 \\ -3 & 4 & -5 \\ 8 & -7 & -9 \end{vmatrix}$$

and delete the column with the z guys...

$$\begin{vmatrix} 2 & -1 & \\ -3 & 4 & \\ 8 & -7 & \end{vmatrix}$$ ← z guys

Replace the column with the "= guys"...

$$D_z = \begin{vmatrix} 2 & -1 & 10 \\ -3 & 4 & 11 \\ 8 & -7 & 12 \end{vmatrix} = 16$$

So, $z = \dfrac{D_z}{D} = \dfrac{16}{-141} = \dfrac{-16}{141}$

So, our final answer is

$$\left(\frac{1499}{141}, \frac{1492}{141}, \frac{-16}{141} \right)$$

Cramer's Rule is great, but crunching a bunch of 3×3 determinants takes a long time and there are only about 6 billion places to make mistakes. on the other hand, doing elimination with messy fractions like these can't be a pretty thing. The moral here is, if the numbers aren't super clean, solving 3x3 is hard!

Your turn (and good luck!)

Solve using Cramer's Rule:

$$2x - 3y \quad = 4$$
$$-x + 4y - z = 1$$
$$6x - 5y + 2z = -3$$

Systems - 3x3's: More Freaky Things

When you're using Cramer's Rule, and you get
$$D = 0$$
for the determinant of the coefficient matrix, it means that there is no nice solution like
$$(-1, \tfrac{2}{3}) \quad \text{or} \quad (4, \tfrac{5}{2}, -3).$$

For 2x2's, it might be that the two lines are parallel... or it might mean that the two equations are the same line.

Unfortunately, you won't be able to tell what the problem is.

It's the same for 3x3's...

If $D = 0$, there won't be a nice solution.
It might be that you've got parallel planes...
or it might be that two or more of the equations are the same plane.

Go back to my previous "FREAKY THINGS" lessons for more details.

It might be that you've got parallel planes...
or it might be that two or more of the equations are the same plane.

Go back to my previous "FREAKY THINGS" lessons for more details.

Are you already in credit card trouble?
Is your FICO score the pits?
Uh... FICO who?
Do you want to learn about this stuff?

Do you want to learn how
to be SMART & RICH?

financeFREAK.com

A fool and his money are soon parted.
Don't be a fool... Be a FREAK!

ARE YOU
TOTALLY
STRESSED OUT?

You don't have to feel out of control. You don't have to feel nervous.
You don't have to feel tired and foggy all the time. Believe me, I've
been there myself. I totally remember what it was like to be a
student -- and I was a student for a LONG time! Since then, I've
been a college teacher so I'm around students all the time - most of
them stressed out. Over the years, I've been teaching my students
how to de-stress and how to deal with stress... I finally decided to
make a stress management site specially designed FOR students --
and anyone else who feels stressed out.

So, settle down and KNOW that you CAN lower your stress! You
really ARE in control of what's going on in your world!
YOU CAN ACTUALLY BE HAPPY AND RELAXED -- yeah, even
while you're a student!

TotallyStressedOut.com
The stress management site for students

FUNCTIONS
-AND-
INVERSE FUNCTIONS

Functions - What's a Function? (Intro to Domain and Range)

This is going to be our first experience with something that's a little more like a concept... But, it's really not that bad. We'll just do a little at a time!

You can think of a function as being a box with a special rule... stuff goes in the box... and stuff comes out of the box.

Let's start with a movie title box:

THE RULE: Spit out the first letter of the movie title. (Only movie titles can go in.)

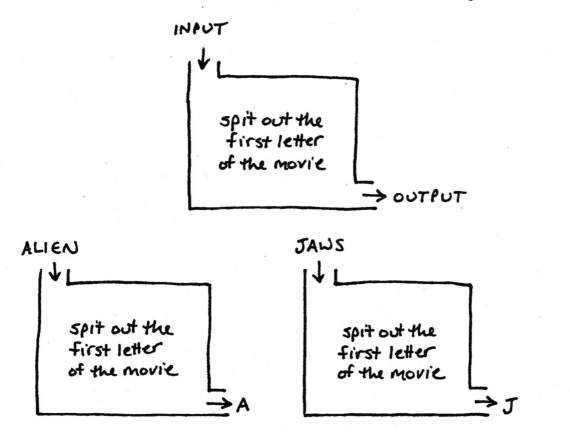

What if we tried this?

101 DALMATIONS

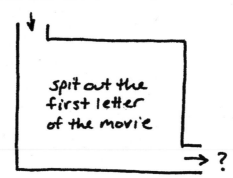

spit out the
first letter
of the movie

→ ?

Hmm... 101 Dalmations starts with a number, not a letter... So, we can't even put it in the box! (Think about it... Where would they have this movie at the video store? Before the A's!)

Here are some official math terms:

The stuff that goes <u>in</u> the box (the <u>input</u>) is called the <u>domain</u>.

The stuff that spits <u>out</u> of the box (the <u>output</u>) is called the <u>range</u>.

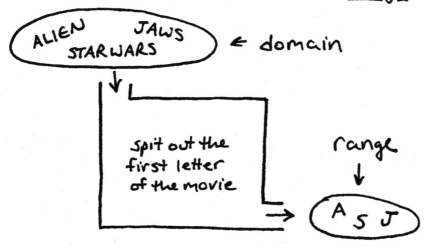

ALIEN   JAWS
STAR WARS   ← domain

spit out the
first letter
of the movie

range

A S J

Domain guys go in... Range guys spit out.
(If you forget the order, it's alphabetical... D→R.)
So, for this box...

domain = all movies that start with a
letter
(101 Dalmations is not in the domain.)

range = the alphabet

And, yes, there are movies for each letter. Here
are some for the weird letters:

Q = Queen Elizabeth (art film)

X = Xanadu (bad disco movie)

Z = Zulu Warriors (pure action!)

Let's try a box with some numbers in it:

THE RULE: Add 1

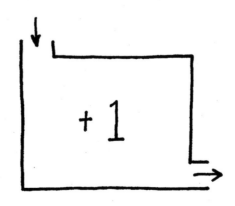

What can we put in this box?

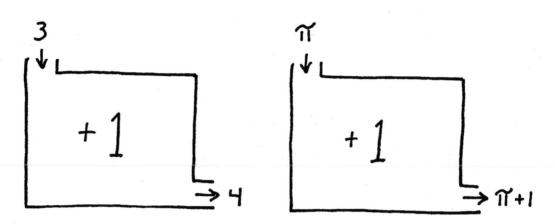

We can put anything in this box -- even goofy irrational numbers like π! So...

$$\text{domain} = \text{all real numbers}$$
$$\text{range} = \text{all real numbers}$$

Try this box:

THE RULE: <u>Square it!</u>
(You figure out the outputs.)

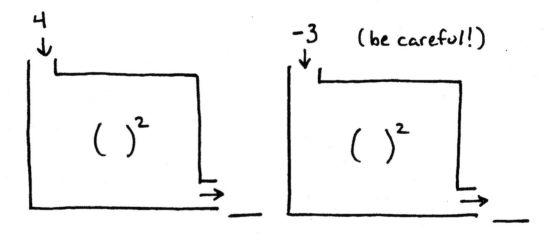

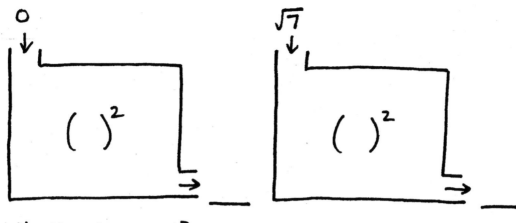

What's the domain?

What's the range?

_____

One last box:

THE RULE: Triple the input, then subtract 5

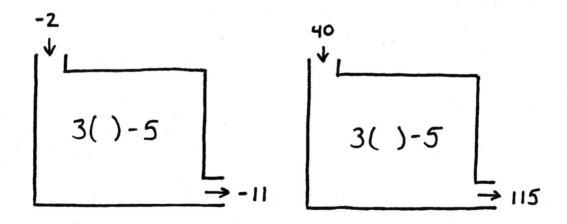

What's the domain and range for this function?

domain = all real numbers

$\quad\quad$ = $(-\infty, \infty)$ ← interval notation

range = $(-\infty, \infty)$

Try it:

What's the domain and range for this function?

THE RULE: Take the square root, then add 4

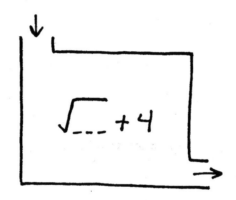

* We're only dealing with real numbers -- no imaginary guys!

Functions - Function Notation

Instead of drawing boxes all the time, we need a way to talk about functions with math symbols.

Let's take a look at a couple of the boxes in our last lesson:

THE RULE: Add 1

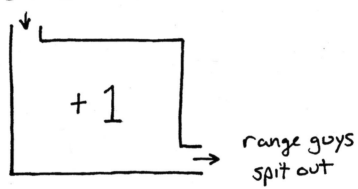

domain guys go in

+ 1

range guys spit out

If we use x to represent our domain guys, here's the official notation:

$$f(x) = \underline{x + 1}$$

input   output

(You read this guy, f(x), as "f of x.")

x guys go in ... and x + 1 guys spit out.

But, x + 1 = f(x)...

So...

x guys go in... and f(x) guys spit out!

(f(x) is just the official output name.)

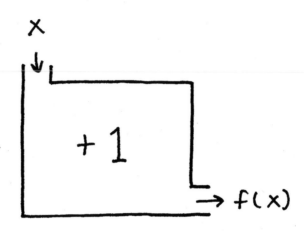

So, this guy...

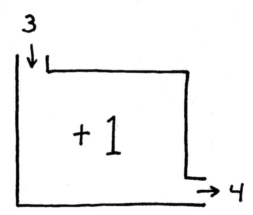

Is officially written as

$$f(3) = 3 + 1 = 4$$
$$f(3) = 4$$

domain
guy

range
guy

What if our input is -5?

$$f(-5) = -5 + 1 = -4$$
$$f(-5) = -4$$

Here's another way to look at it:

we started with $f(x) = x+1$...
$f(-5)$ is like saying "let $x = -5$."

What about this box?

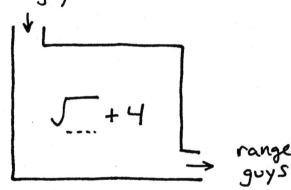

The official notation would be

$$f(x) = \sqrt{x} + 4$$

x guys   and this
go in   spits out

So, $f(9) = \sqrt{9} + 4 = 3 + 4 = 7$

like letting $x = 9$

Your turn!

Find the official notation for this box, then use the notation to find

$$f(0)$$
$$f(6)$$
$$f(-3)$$

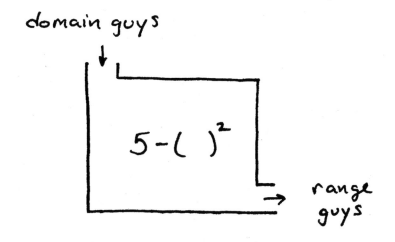

If we've got the picture of a critter (i.e. the graph), there's an easy way to tell if it's a function or not.

It's called <u>The Vertical Line Test</u>:

> If you can draw a vertical line anywhere on a graph so that it hits the graph in more than one spot, then the graph is <u>not</u> a function.

Check out Standard Parabola Guy:

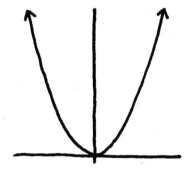

No matter where we drop a vertical line, it only hits the parabola in one spot.

So, Standard Parabola Guy is a function!

$$f(x) = x^2$$

a number goes in

and it's square spits out

What about a parabola lying on its side?
(I'll teach you about these later.)

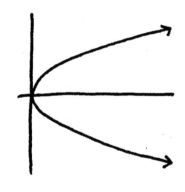 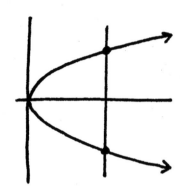

Ouch! This guy hits in two spots!

So, Sideways Parabola Guy is not a function.

The only problem with this method is that you don't always have a picture to look at.

(There are other ways to tell that I'll show you later.)

Which of these are functions?

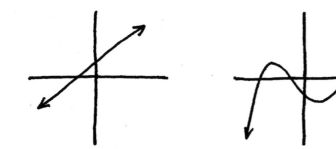 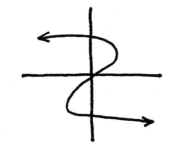

The first two are... The first guy is just a line. He's officially called a linear function.

What's the only type of line that isn't a function?

The second guy passes the vertical line test, so it's a function.

The last guy fails the vertical line test and is not a function.

Your turn!

Which of these are functions?

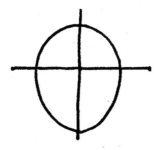 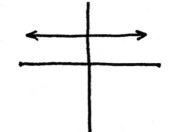 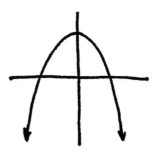

Which of these are functions? Draw rough
sketches of the graphs so you can do the
vertical line test:

$$y = \frac{-2}{3}x + 4$$

$$y = 5x - x^2$$

What about these?

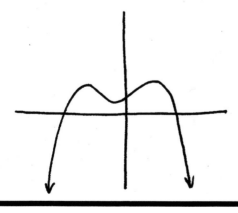

Functions - With Sets

Sometimes we (math geeks) like to mess around with sets of points like

$$\{(1,2), (2,4), (3,2)\}$$

This set is a rule -- just like our boxes were.

$$Rule = \{(1,2), (2,4), (3,2)\}$$

These guys in the set are just like (x,y) points on a graph...

So, we can actually graph this thing:

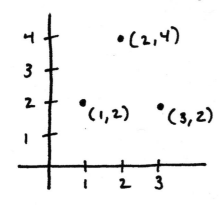

* Don't connect the dots!
  These are isolated
  points and this isn't
  a coloring book!

Just like before, the x guys are our input guys -- the domain:

$$R = \{(1,2), (2,4), (3,2)\}$$

domain guy   domain guy   domain guy

And remember that y guys are really f(x) guys--
range guys:

$$R = \{ (1,2), (2,4), (3,2) \}$$

range   range   range
guy   guy   guy

OK, so how can I tell if this guy is a function or not? There are two ways: The old vertical line test and a new way that uses domain and range blobs.

Here's the vertical line test way -- but, now I want to be sophisticated and use the official definition:

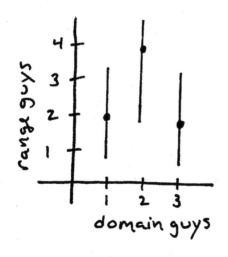

Yes, R is a function since each element in the domain goes to exactly one element in the range.
(It passes the vertical line test.)

Your turn!

Is $R = \{ (a,1), (b,1), (c,2), (b,3) \}$ a function? (There's room on the next page.)

* put the letters along the bottom since they are
the domain guys!

_____

Is this a function?

$$R = \{ (1, b), (2, a), (3, a), (4, c) \}$$

* now the numbers go along the bottom!

Functions - Domain and Range

Remember that domain guys are all the x's that you are allowed to put into a function... and the range guys are all the guys that get spit out of the function:

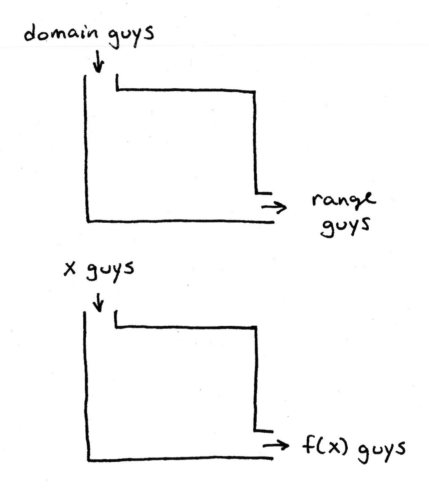

And remember that

$$f(x) \text{ is just another name for } y!$$

Now, I want to look more at graphs, so let's look at this like

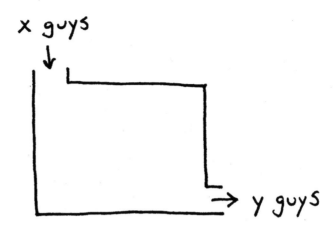

x guys

y guys

Let's look at Standard Parabola Guy:

$$y = x^2$$

Before we look at the graph, let's think about it again...

What x guys are we allowed to put into this thing?

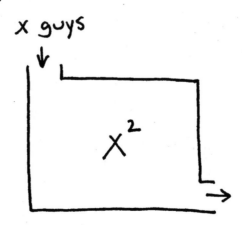

x guys

x^2

We can square anything!

$$(-3)^2 = 9 \qquad 0^2 = 0 \qquad 5^2 = 25 \qquad 3.1^2 = 9.61$$

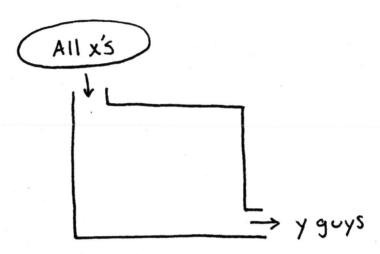

So, what kind of y guys come out?

Squares are never negative!

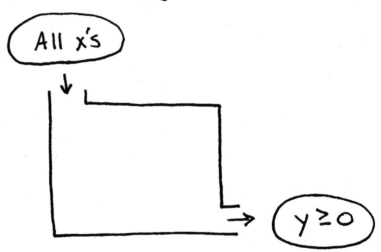

Let's use this to make a connection with the graph of Standard Parabola Guy:

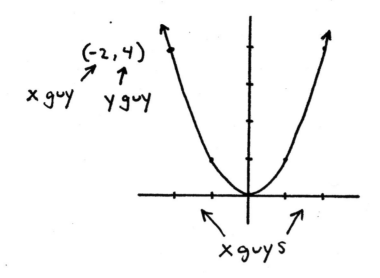

(-2, 4)

x guy   y guy

x guys

Notice that this parabola gets wider and wider...
Eventually, if we kept drawing, _all x's_ would be
involved in the graph.

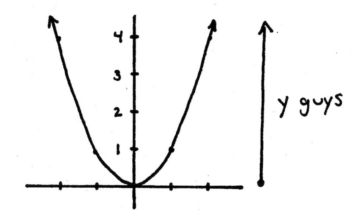

y guys

And notice that the y guys go from zero up.
This matches up with our function box thinking!

$$\text{domain} = (-\infty, \infty)$$

$$\text{range} = [0, \infty)$$

Let's look at another one:

Let's find the domain and range of this guy:

$$y = -x^2 + 3$$

Hmm... Well, I can't think of any x's that can't be put into this thing... But, what about the range? We really need to graph it.

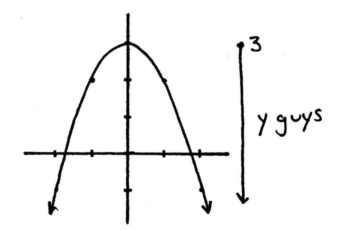

Again, the domain will be all x's (since he spreads out forever). And the range goes from 3 down...

$$\text{domain} = (-\infty, \infty)$$
$$\text{range} = (-\infty, 3]$$

Try it:

From the graph of $y = x^2 - 4$, find the domain and range.

Now that you get the idea, can you figure out the domain and range of this thing?

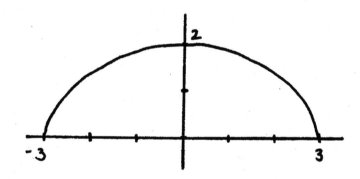

What x guys are involved?

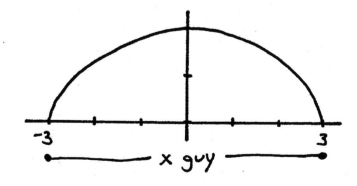

So, the domain is

$$[-3, 3]$$

What y guys are involved?

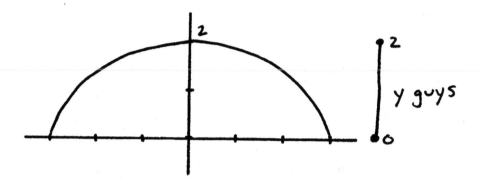

So, the range is

$$[0, 2]$$

Your turn:

Find the domain and range:

(By the way, this thing isn't a function, is it?)

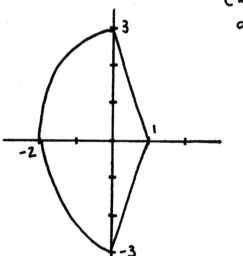

Functions - Domains (Flying Blind)

OK, so suppose we don't have the graph of a function to look at like in the last section... Can we still find the domain and range?

Domains: Yes (as long as the algebra doesn't get too hairy... and it won't for us)

Ranges: Not really (you usually need the picture -- unless it's something really basic.)

So, we'll just be doing domains on these -- which is really where the action is anyway.

Asking for the domain of a function is the same as asking

"What are all the possible x guys that I can stick into this thing?"

Sometimes, what you'll really be looking for is

"Is there anything I <u>can't</u> stick in?"

Check it out:

Let's find the domain of $f(x) = \dfrac{2}{x-3}$

Do you see any x guys that would cause a problem here?

What about x = 3?

$$f(3) = \frac{2}{3-3} = \frac{2}{0} \leftarrow \text{ouch!}$$

So, x = 3 is a bad guy! Everyone else is ok though.

The domain is all real numbers except 3.

What would the interval notation be?

When in doubt, graph it on a number line:

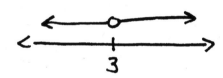

Do the interval notation in two pieces:

$$\text{domain} = (-\infty, 3) \cup (3, \infty)$$

Your turn:

Find the domain of $f(x) = \dfrac{5}{x+7}$

Sometimes, you can't find the domain with a quick look.

Check it out:

Let's find the domain of $f(x) = \dfrac{1}{3-2x}$

Hmm... It's not so obvious!

But, we are still looking for the same thing:

$$f(x) = \dfrac{1}{3-2x} \quad \leftarrow \quad \text{The bad } x \text{ that makes the denominator 0!}$$

How do we find it? Easy!

Set the denominator = 0 and solve!

$$3 - 2x = 0$$
$$\underline{-3 \qquad\qquad -3}$$
$$-2x = -3$$
$$x = \dfrac{-3}{-2} = \dfrac{3}{2}$$

The domain is $\left(-\infty, \dfrac{3}{2}\right) \cup \left(\dfrac{3}{2}, \infty\right)$.

Try it:

Find the domain of $f(x) = \dfrac{6}{5x+3}$ * show work!!

How about this one?

$$f(x) = \sqrt{x+5}$$

Square roots -- what do we know about square roots?

$\sqrt{16} = 4$ ... So, 16 is OK to put in.

$\sqrt{0} = 0$ ... So, 0 is OK.

$\sqrt{3.2} \approx 1.788...$ Yuck! But, 3.2 is OK.

$\sqrt{-25} = ?$ ... Nope! Can't do it! *We only want real numbers!

No negatives are OK!

$$\sqrt{inside}$$
↗

The inside of a radical cannot be negative if we want real answers only (no i guys). So, the inside of a radical has to be 0 or a positive number.

Set inside ≥ 0 and solve it!

Now, let's find the domain of

$$f(x) = \sqrt{x+5}$$

$$x + 5 \geq 0$$

$$x \geq -5$$

So, the domain of $f(x) = \sqrt{x+5}$ is $[-5, \infty)$.

Try it:

Find the domain of $f(x) = \sqrt{3-x}$ * show work!

Here's a messier one:

Let's find the domain of $f(x) = \sqrt{7-8x}$

Set $7-8x \geq 0$ and solve!

$$7-8x \geq 0$$
$$\underline{-7 \qquad\qquad -7}$$
$$-8x \geq -7$$
$$\frac{-8x}{-8} \leq \frac{-7}{-8}$$
$$x \leq \frac{7}{8}$$

The domain is $\left(-\infty, \frac{7}{8}\right]$.

Your turn:

Find the domain of $f(x) = \sqrt{4x-5}$ * show work!

Functions - Messier Notation

OK, so we're cool with the easy notation like

$$f(x) = x^2 + 5$$

So $f(3) = (3)^2 + 5 = 9 + 5 = 14$

$$f(-2) = (-2)^2 + 5 = 4 + 5 = 9$$

These ( ) are killer important!

What if we let $x = k$?

We'd get $f(k) = k^2 + 5$

That wasn't so bad... but, they get worse!

What would $f(x+h)$ be?

Let's get your brain thinking the right way...
then it will be easy!

$$f(x) = x^2 + 5$$

Think of it as

$$f(blob) = (blob)^2 + 5$$

This function guy takes any blob... squares it...
then adds 5! So...

$$f(karen) = (karen)^2 + 5$$
$$f(coolmath) = (coolmath)^2 + 5$$

$$f(booger) = (booger)^2 + 5$$

$$f(x+h) = (x+h)^2 + 5$$

Whoa, dude! You just got tricked into doing one of the hardest things in Algebra!

$$\text{If } f(x) = x^2 + 5$$

$$\text{then } f(x+h) = (x+h)^2 + 5 \qquad \text{clean it up!}$$

$$= x^2 + 2xh + h^2 + 5$$

What about this one?

$$\text{If } f(x) = 3x - 2x^2$$

Find $f(blob)$:

$$f(blob) = 3(blob) - 2(blob)^2$$

Find $f(zebra)$:

$$f(zebra) = 3(zebra) - 2(zebra)^2$$

Find $f(x+h)$:

$$f(x+h) = 3(x+h) - 2(x+h)^2$$

See how important these ( ) are?

$$= 3x + 3h - 2(x^2 + 2xh + h^2)$$

$$= 3x + 3h - 2x^2 - 4xh - 2h^2$$

Always do the blob thing and use ( ) and you'll never go wrong!

Try it!

$$\text{If } f(x) = 4x^2 - x$$

Find $f(blob)$:

Find $f(x+h)$:

Functions - The Difference Quotient

OK, so why did I get such a charge out of finding $f(x+h)$ in the last lesson?

Because it shows up in a formula that is super important in Calculus!

The Difference Quotient:
$$\frac{f(x+h) - f(x)}{h}$$

So, you're going to be given a function like
$$f(x) = x+2$$

and you'll need to work out that big mess. It's not that bad once you get the hang of it.

It's just three pieces:

① $f(x+h)$ which we can now do!

② $-f(x)$ Easy - just remember to use ( )!

③ $\frac{}{h}$ Piece of cake!

Let's work this guy out:
$$f(x) = x+2$$

① $f(x+h)$:

Do the blob thang! $f(blob) = (blob) + 2$

So $f(x+h) = (x+h) + 2$

$\qquad = x+h+2$ ← we don't need the ( ) here.

② $-f(x)$:

This is just subtracting the original function

$-(x+2)$

↖ ( ) is important!

③ Just stick an h under everything and clean up that bad boy!

Here we go!

$$\frac{f(x+h) - f(x)}{h} = \frac{\overset{\swarrow f(x+h)}{[x+h+2]} - \overset{\swarrow f(x)}{(x+2)}}{h} \quad \text{clean it up!}$$

$$= \frac{x+h+2-x-2}{h} = \frac{h}{h} = 1$$

Let's do another one:

Given $f(x) = 2x^2 + 3$ find the difference quotient:

Do the blob thang:

$$f(blob) = 2(blob)^2 + 3$$

$$\frac{f(x+h) - f(x)}{h} = \frac{[2(x+h)^2 + 3] - (2x^2 + 3)}{h}$$

f(x+h) ↙   ↙ f(x)

$$= \frac{2(x^2 + 2xh + h^2) + 3 - 2x^2 - 3}{h}$$

$$= \frac{2x^2 + 4xh + 2h^2 + 3 - 2x^2 - 3}{h} = \frac{4xh + 2h^2}{h}$$

$$= \frac{h(4x + 2h)}{h} = 4x + 2h$$

↖ At this point, everything without an h should subtract out!

↑
* If you do these correctly, this h will reduce out at the end!

Your turn!

Given $f(x) = 5 - 3x$ find the difference quotient:

Given $f(x) = 8 - 3x^2$ find the difference quotient:

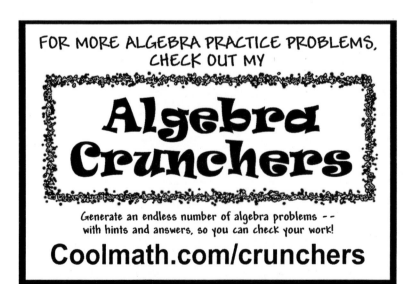

Inverse Functions - What Are They and What Do They Do?

Inverse functions undo each other!

That's it. Go home.

OK. I'll elaborate

Think of a number... I'll wait.

OK, now add 3 to it... Now, subtract 3 from that. What do you get?

The number you started with!

check it out:

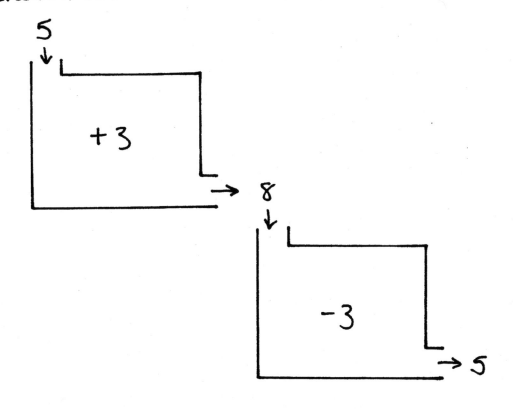

So, these guys are inverse functions:

$$f(x) = x + 3 \qquad\qquad g(x) = x - 3$$

add the 3 on...   takes the 3 off

Let's do another one:

Think of a number -- make it positive...

Now, square it ... Then, take the square root of that. What do you get?

The number you started with!

Check it out:

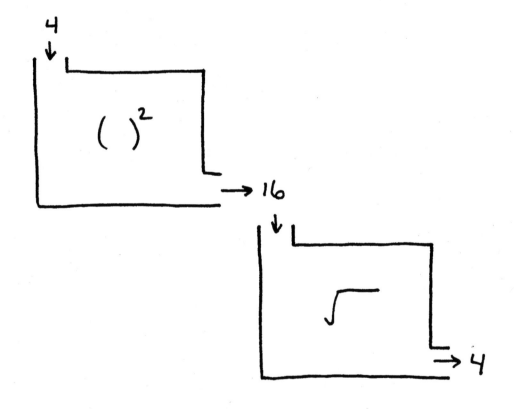

So, these guys are inverse functions:

$$f(x) = x^2 \qquad g(x) = \sqrt{x}$$

What if we try sticking a negative number in?

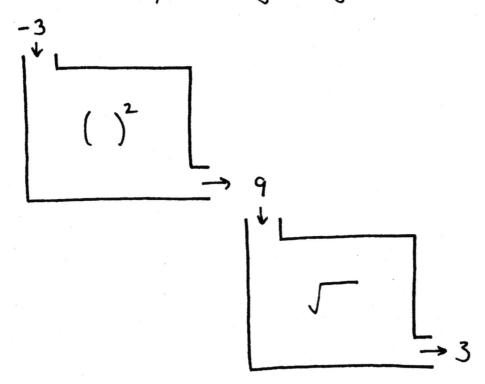

A −3 went in... but, a 3 came out! These don't work for negative numbers. So, for this one, we have to say

These are inverse functions only when $x \geq 0$:

$$f(x) = x^2 \qquad g(x) = \sqrt{x}$$

(This will be even clearer later.)

The official notation for the inverse function of a guy named $f(x)$ is

$$f^{-1}(x)$$

(read as "f inverse of x.")

* The little "-1" is <u>not</u> an exponent! It's just a notation. Hey -- they didn't ask <u>me</u> about this stuff when they made it up!

I know you're really excited about this... But, you don't know enough to try any problems yet. Keep reading!

Inverse Functions - The Picture - Two Big Things to Know

Let's graph the inverse functions we had in the last lesson on the same graph and see what happens:

$$f(x) = x + 3 \text{ and } g(x) = x - 3$$

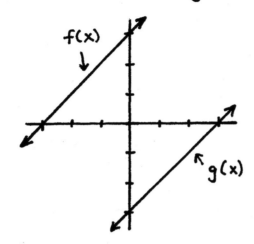

There are two big things I want you to notice:

①

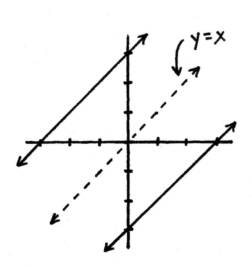

They are mirror images over the line $y = x$.

(In other words, they are symmetric with respect to the line $y = x$.)

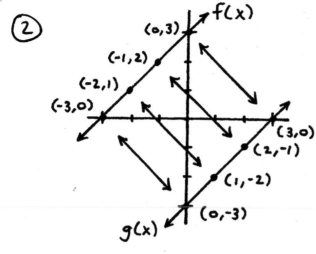

② f(x)
(0,3)
(-1,2)
(-2,1)
(-3,0)
(3,0)
(2,-1)
(1,-2)
(0,-3)
g(x)

Notice that every point on f(x) has a reversed partner on g(x).

(0, 3) has (3, 0) as a partner and so on.

So, just remember this:

Every (x, y) has a (y, x) partner.

Let's look at another example:
With the two previous things in mind, can you draw the inverse of this?

$$g(x) = \sqrt{x}$$

Since we don't know what the graph of $g(x) = \sqrt{x}$ looks like yet (well, I do... but, you don't), let's plot a few points:

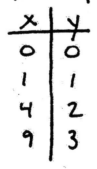

x	y
0	0
1	1
4	2
9	3

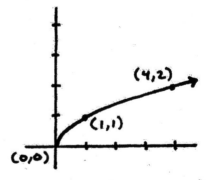

(4,2)
(1,1)
(0,0)

It's just half a parabola lying on its side!

Cool! So, what are the two things?

① symmetric with respect to y=x
② every (x,y) has a (y,x) partner

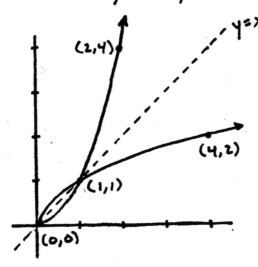

Hey! It's half of standard Parabola Guy!

$$f(x) = x^2$$

Now, I can tell you why I said x≥0 for these guys in the last lesson

$$f(x) = x^2 \quad \text{and} \quad g(x) = \sqrt{x}$$

If we drew the whole parabola...

and flipped him over the line y=x using the "every (x,y) has a (y,x)" thing...

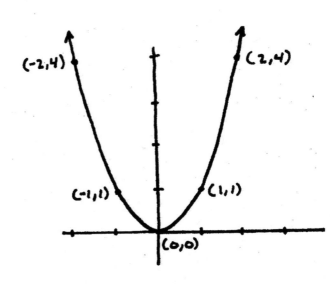

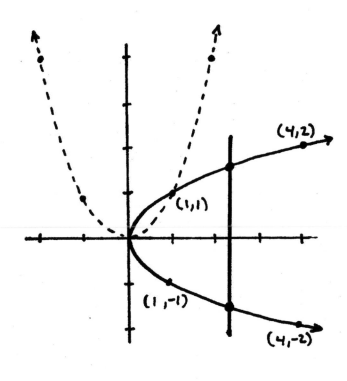

(4,2)

(1,1)

(1,-1)

(4,-2)

The result would fail the vertical line test. It's <u>not</u> a function!

And what's the name of this chapter?

Inverse <u>Functions</u>!

We only care about them if they are functions.

(Harsh, but true.)

Your turn!

Graph the inverse of this function:

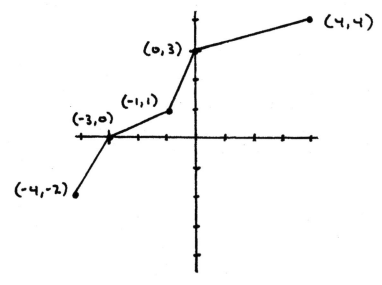

(4,4)

(0,3)

(-1,1)

(-3,0)

(-4,-2)

There is an algebra test to see if two functions are inverses of each other. But, before I can tell you about it, I need to show you this stuff first.

This notation we know:

$$f(x) = x^2 + 3$$

And we think of it as:

$$f(blob) = (blob)^2 + 3$$

Now, we're going to have two functions to mess with at once ... Like these:

$$f(x) = x^2 + 3 \quad and \quad g(x) = x - 2$$

The game is that we'll need to find

$$f(g(x))$$

That's f of g(x).

If you read it and say it correctly, it's really going to help you do the problem!

Before, we had f(x) which we read as " f of x"...

Now, we have f(g(x))...

f of g(x)

Same game... Just a bigger blob!

Here's $f(x)$ again, it case you forgot:
$$f(x) = x^2 + 3$$
Remember the blob game:
$$f(blob) = (blob)^2 + 3$$
So, for $f(g(x))$... our blob is $g(x)$...
$$f(g(x)) = (g(x))^2 + 3$$

There's more to the problem and we aren't finished, but I'm going to linger here for a bit because I know that this can get confusing if you jump in too quickly.

Let's look at another one...
$$\text{Given } f(x) = 5x - 3$$
Here's $f(blob)$:
$$f(blob) = 5(blob) - 3$$
Here's $f(g(x))$:
$$f(g(x)) = 5(g(x)) - 3$$

One more:
$$\text{Given } f(x) = 7x^2 - x + 3$$
$$f(blob) = 7(blob)^2 - (blob) + 3$$
These ( ) will be really important!

$$f(g(x)) = 7(g(x))^2 - (g(x)) + 3$$

Try it:

Given $f(x) = x^3 - 6x^2 - 5$

$f(blob) =$

$f(g(x)) =$

---

ok, so, what if you had this:

$$f(x) = 2x^2 + 5$$

$$f(blob) = 2(blob)^2 + 5$$

Now, what if I told you to replace the word "blob" with "x+3?"

$$blob = x + 3$$

$$f(blob) = 2(blob)^2 + 5$$

$$f(x+3) = 2(x+3)^2 + 5$$

This is the game! First, we do the blob thing. Then, we get with the notation and put the $g(x)$ in... Then, we replace that $g(x)$ with whatever $g(x)$ really is. Don't worry. It's easy! Check this out:

Given $f(x) = 6x + 1$ and $g(x) = 2x^2 + 5$

Find $f(g(x))$:

   ① Find $f(blob)$:

      $f(blob) = 6(blob) + 1$

   ② Find $f(g(x))$:

      $f(g(x)) = 6(g(x)) + 1$

   ③ Replace the $g(x)$ with $2x^2 + 5$

      since $g(x) = 2x^2 + 5$

   $f(2x^2 + 5) = 6(2x^2 + 5) + 1$

Yeah, this is the answer, but we always clean it up to be polite.

$f(2x^2 + 5) = 12x^2 + 30 + 1 = 12x^2 + 31$

Here's another one — let's do the guy we started before:

   Given $f(x) = x^2 + 3$ and $g(x) = x - 2$

   Find $f(g(x))$

   ① $f(blob) = (blob)^2 + 3$

   ② $f(g(x)) = (g(x))^2 + 3$

   ③ $f(x-2) = (x-2)^2 + 3$

        $= x^2 - 4x + 4 + 3 = x^2 - 4x + 7$

Your turn:

Given $f(x) = 5x^2 + x$ and $g(x) = 3x - 1$
Find $f(g(x))$

By the way, the official math notation for

$$f(g(x)) \text{ is } (f \circ g)(x)$$

This little guy here is <u>not</u> a multiplication dot. I like to think of it as a little "o" for "of." f <u>of</u> $g(x)$

Why do we use this notation? So that everyone thinks we're doing something really hard and that we are super smart.

We can flip this all around too! We've been finding $(f \circ g)(x)$ which is $f(g(x))$...

But, if that wasn't exciting enough (try to calm down), we can find

$$(g \circ f)(x)!$$ Dang!

Check it out:

Given $f(x) = 6x + 1$ and $g(x) = 2x^2 + 5$

Let's find $(g \circ f)(x)$ ... which is $g(f(x))$

① $g(blob) = 2(blob)^2 + 5$

② $g(f(x)) = 2(f(x))^2 + 5$

③ $g(6x+1) = 2(6x+1)^2 + 5$
$$= 2(36x^2 + 12x + 1) + 5$$
$$= 72x^2 + 24x + 7$$

We found $(f \circ g)(x)$ a couple pages ago:

$$(f \circ g)(x) = 12x^2 + 31$$

and $(g \circ f)(x) = 72x^2 + 24x + 7$

Notice that $(f \circ g)(x) \neq (g \circ f)(x)$!

Usually, you <u>will</u> get two different things. That's why it's so important to read the notation the right way... or you may end up doing it backwards!

Preview: If two functions are inverses of each other, you <u>will</u> get the same thing for both!

Here's another one we looked at before:

Given $f(x) = x^2 + 3$ and $g(x) = x - 2$

Find $(g \circ f)(x) \ldots$ which is $g(f(x))$

① $g(blob) = (blob) - 2$

② $g(f(x)) = (f(x)) - 2$

③ $g(x^2+3) = (x^2+3) - 2$

$\qquad = x^2 + 1$

$(f \circ g)(x) = x^2 - 4x + 7 \neq x^2 + 1 = (g \circ f)(x)$

Try it:

Given $f(x) = 5x^2 + x$ and $g(x) = 3x - 1$

Find $(g \circ f)(x)$

Look back a couple of pages...
What did you get for $(f \circ g)(x)$?

Inverse Functions - How to Tell If Two Functions are Inverses

So, how do we check to see if two functions are inverses of each other?

Well, we learned before, that we can look at the graphs. Remember, if the two graphs are symmetric with respect to the line $y=x$ (mirror images over $y=x$), then they are inverse functions.

But, we need a way to check without the graphs, because we won't always know what the graphs look like!

So, just crunching some Algebra, here's one way to look at it:

If you've got two functions, $f(x)$ and $g(x)$, and
$$(f \circ g)(x) = (g \circ f)(x)$$
then $f(x)$ and $g(x)$ are inverse functions.

Let's try this on an easy one that we know will work:

$$f(x) = x+3 \text{ and } g(x) = x-3$$

$\boxed{1}$ $(f \circ g)(x) = f(g(x))$

① $f(blob) = (blob) + 3$

② $f(g(x)) = (g(x)) + 3$

③ $f(x-3) = (x-3) + 3 = x$

2 $(g \circ f)(x) = g(f(x))$

① $g(\text{blob}) = (\text{blob}) - 3$

② $g(f(x)) = (f(x)) - 3$

③ $g(x+3) = (x+3) - 3 = x$

So, $(f \circ g)(x) = x$ and $(g \circ f)(x) = x$

$$(f \circ g)(x) = (g \circ f)(x)$$

Yep, they are inverses, just like we thought!

Let's do another easy one we already know:

$$f(x) = x^2 \text{ and } g(x) = \sqrt{x}$$
for $x \geq 0$

1 $(f \circ g)(x) = f(g(x))$

① $f(\text{blob}) = (\text{blob})^2$

② $f(g(x)) = (g(x))^2$

③ $f(\sqrt{x}) = (\sqrt{x})^2 = x$

2 $(g \circ f)(x) = g(f(x))$

① $g(\text{blob}) = \sqrt{\text{blob}}$

② $g(f(x)) = \sqrt{f(x)}$

③ $g(x^2) = \sqrt{x^2} = x$

Uh... Did you notice something weird too?

We got x's again.

That's no coincidence, Baby!

> If $(f \circ g)(x) = x$ or $(g \circ f)(x) = x$, then $f(x)$ and $g(x)$ are inverse functions.

So, you really only need to check one of them!
Check it out:

Are these inverse functions?

$$f(x) = 2x - 5 \quad \text{and} \quad g(x) = \tfrac{1}{2}x + \tfrac{5}{2}$$

$$(f \circ g)(x) = f(g(x))$$

① $f(blob) = 2(blob) - 5$

② $f(g(x)) = 2(g(x)) - 5$

③ $f\left(\tfrac{1}{2}x + \tfrac{5}{2}\right) = 2\left(\tfrac{1}{2}x + \tfrac{5}{2}\right) - 5$

$$= x + 5 - 5 = x \quad \boxed{\text{Yep!}}$$

You can double-check it by crunching $(g \circ f)(x)$.

Your turn:

Are these inverse functions?
$$f(x) = x^2 - 3 \text{ and } g(x) = \sqrt{x+3}$$

Are these inverse functions?
$$f(x) = 2x - 5 \text{ and } g(x) = \tfrac{1}{2}x + 5$$

Inverse Functions - How to Find the Inverse

This is easy -- it's just a list of steps. At this level, the problems are pretty simple.

Let's just do one, then I'll write out the list of steps for you.

Find the inverse of $f(x) = -\frac{1}{3}x + 1$

STEP 1: Stick a "y" in for the "f(x)" guy:

$$y = -\frac{1}{3}x + 1$$

STEP 2: Switch the x and y (because every (x,y) has a (y,x) partner!):

$$x = -\frac{1}{3}y + 1$$

STEP 3: Solve for y:

$$x = -\frac{1}{3}y + 1 \qquad \text{multiply by 3 to ditch the fraction}$$

$$\begin{array}{cc} 3x = -y + 3 & \text{ditch the +3} \\ \underline{-3 \qquad\quad -3} & \\ 3x - 3 = -y & \text{multiply by -1} \end{array}$$

$$-3x + 3 = y \quad \rightarrow \quad y = -3x + 3$$

STEP 4: Stick in the inverse notation, $f^{-1}(x)$:

$$f^{-1}(x) = -3x + 3$$

Remember, you've got two ways you can double-check this answer to see if it's right:

① Graph $f(x)$ and $f^{-1}(x)$ on the same graph and see if they're mirror images over the line $y=x$. (Easy — since these are both lines.)

Do it!

② Find either $(f \circ g)(x)$ or $(g \circ f)(x)$: (or both for practice!)

ok, here's the list of steps:

How to find the inverse of a function:

STEP 1: Stick a "y" in for the "f(x)".

STEP 2: Switch the x and y.

STEP 3: Solve for y.

STEP 4: Stick "$f^{-1}(x)$" in for the "y".

THEN, CHECK IT!

Here's another one:

Find the inverse of $f(x) = 2x - 1$

STEP 1: $\quad y = 2x - 1$

STEP 2: $\quad x = 2y - 1$

STEP 3:

$$x = 2y - 1$$
$$\underline{+1 \qquad\quad +1}$$
$$x + 1 = 2y$$
$$\frac{x+1}{2} = \frac{2y}{2}$$
$$\tfrac{1}{2}x + \tfrac{1}{2} = y$$

STEP 4: $\quad f^{-1}(x) = \tfrac{1}{2}x + \tfrac{1}{2}$

Check it!

_____

Your turn:

Find the inverse of $f(x) = -\frac{2}{3}x + 5$

Are you already in credit card trouble?
Is your FICO score the pits?
Uh... FICO who?
Do you want to learn about this stuff?

Do you want to learn how to be SMART & RICH?

financeFREAK.com

A fool and his money are soon parted.
Don't be a fool... Be a FREAK!

ARE YOU TOTALLY STRESSED OUT?

You don't have to feel out of control. You don't have to feel nervous. You don't have to feel tired and foggy all the time. Believe me, I've been there myself. I totally remember what it was like to be a student -- and I was a student for a LONG time! Since then, I've been a college teacher so I'm around students all the time - most of them stressed out. Over the years, I've been teaching my students how to de-stress and how to deal with stress... I finally decided to make a stress management site specially designed FOR students -- and anyone else who feels stressed out.

So, settle down and KNOW that you CAN lower your stress! You really ARE in control of what's going on in your world! YOU CAN ACTUALLY BE HAPPY AND RELAXED -- yeah, even while you're a student!

TotallyStressedOut.com
The stress management site for students

EXPONENTIALS
-AND-
LOGARITHMS

Exponentials - The Exponential Monster

Here's the situation:

Your spaceship has crashed on an unknown planet. You and your crew encounter a drooling carnivorous alien monster. As you can guess, this is not good. It gets worse. While you are cowering in a cave, trying not to cry "mommy" in front of your crew, your science officer is able to chart the monster's growth over several hours time. She comes back to you with her report (and minus one arm). The news is grim... With each hour that passes, the monster doubles in size (specifically, his height.) (She also said that the monster's stomach was making those growly-hungry noises.)

If we assume that the monster is 1 foot tall at birth, what formula would describe the growth of the monster?

Well, let's figure it out. The best thing to do to figure out things like this is to make a chart of data. You can usually find a pattern that will lead to the formula!

TIME (t)	HEIGHT IN FEET
At birth: $t=0$	1
After 1 hour: $t=1$	$1 \cdot 2 = 2$
After 2 hours: $t=2$	$1 \cdot 2 \cdot 2 = 2^2 = 4$
After 3 hours: $t=3$	$1 \cdot 2 \cdot 2 \cdot 2 = 2^3 = 8$
After 4 hours: $t=4$	$1 \cdot 2 \cdot 2 \cdot 2 \cdot 2 = 2^4 = 16$

See a pattern yet?

$\vdots$

After 10 hours: $t=10$	$2^{10} = 1024$

$\vdots$

After t hours	2^t

We can even rewrite the first line of the table like this so the pattern sticks:

At birth: $t=0$ $\qquad\qquad\qquad$ $1 = 2^0$

We can write

$$\text{height} = 2^t$$

Using function notation, our official formula is

$$h(t) = 2^t$$

$\nearrow$ h for height $\qquad\nwarrow$ t is our input variable

Now, you can figure out the monster's height at any time!

How tall will one of these monsters be 6 hours and 30 minutes after it's born?

That's $t = 6.5...$

$$h(t) = 2^t$$
$$h(6.5) = 2^{6.5} \approx 90.5$$

After 6.5 hours, the monster will be about 90.5 feet tall.

(I'm sure you can only imagine the amount of drool something that big would produce... And how hungry it would be!)

Your turn:

How tall would the monster be 4.7 hours after birth?

How tall would the monster be 3.2 hours after birth?

By the way, this thing

$$h(t) = 2^t$$

is called an "exponential" since the variable is up in the exponent.

$$h(t) = 2^t \leftarrow$$

↑ The 2 is called the "base."

Before this, we were working with guys like

$$f(x) = x^2$$

↖

where the variable is downstairs in the base.

Back to the story:

For some reason, your science officer starts yelling crazy things at you (while waving her one arm all around) and quits. In desperation, you promote the crew cook, Stu, and send him out of the cave to do more exploring. Unfortunately, he finds a second species of drooling alien monster... Fortunately for Stu, it's an herbavore! Unfortunately for Stu, your uniforms are green. Days later, one of Stu's socks and a clip board of growth data for the monster is found.

Here's what Stu had written:

SECOND ALIEN SPECIES IS 4 INCHES TALL AT BIRTH

TIME (t)	HEIGHT IN INCHES
At birth: $t = 0$	4
After 1 hour: $t = 1$	$4 \cdot 3 = 12$
After 2 hours: $t = 2$	$4 \cdot 3 \cdot 3 = 4 \cdot 3^2 = 36$
After 3 hours: $t = 3$	$4 \cdot 3 \cdot 3 \cdot 3 = 4 \cdot 3^3 = 108$
After 4 hours: $t = 4$	$4 \cdot 3 \cdot 3 \cdot 3 \cdot 3 = 4 \cdot 3^4 = 324$
$\vdots$	
After 10 hours: $t = 10$	$4 \cdot 3^{10}$
$\vdots$	
After t hours	$4 \cdot 3^t$

$4 \cdot 3^t$ ← time

↗ initial height

↑ growth rate

CONCLUSION: WITH EACH HOUR THAT PASSES, THE MONSTER TRIPLES IN HEIGHT AND MAY BE TASTY BROILED WITH ONIONS.

FORMULA FOR GROWTH:

$$h(t) = 4 \cdot 3^t$$

Your turn:

How tall will this species of monster be after 2.5 hours?

After 4.2 hours?

You are sent out of the cave next... You find a third species of alien monster. It's not drooling, but it does have a serious breath problem. You find that this species is 2 cm tall at birth and gets five times as tall with each day that passes.

Create a formula to describe the monster's growth:

How tall will the monster be after 3.7 days?

Exponentials - Alien Amoebas

Going from large to small, you find another type of critter on the planet: alien ameobas! Since you're stranded on the planet and there's nothing else to do except run screaming from some of the inhabitants, you decide to study amoeba populations.

Typical animal populations grow by mommy and daddy animals making baby animals. (Hey-- this book is G rated!) Amoeba populations, on the other hand, grow by each amoeba splitting into two amoebas.

So, if each alien amoeba splits into 2 amoebas every hour, can we create a formula to describe the growth of the amoeba population?

Let's say we start with 50 amoebas...

TIME (t)	POPULATION
start: $t = 0$	50
after 1 hour: $t = 1$	$50 \cdot 2 = 100$
after 2 hours: $t = 2$	$50 \cdot 2 \cdot 2 = 50 \cdot 2^2 = 200$
after 3 hours: $t = 3$	$50 \cdot 2 \cdot 2 \cdot 2 = 50 \cdot 2^3 = 400$

Look familiar?

after t hours

$$50 \cdot 2^t$$

initial population → $50 \cdot 2^t$ ← number of splits

↑ split factor

Hey! This is just like alien monster growth!

OK, so, what if it gets more complicated?

What if the amoeba doesn't make a complete split in one hour? What if it only makes part of the split in an hour?

Let's say that a certain alien amoeba splits into 1.25 amoebas each hour... If we start with 37 amoebas, how many will there be in 6 hours?

First, we need to get our growth formula:

Our split factor is 1.25...

our initial population is 37...

The number of splits is 6...

$$\text{number of amoebas} = 37 \cdot 1.25^{6} \; \leftarrow \text{number of splits}$$

initial population → split factor

$$\text{number of amoebas} \approx 141.14$$

Try it!

If we start with 153 alien amoebas and each amoeba splits into 2.4 amoebas each hour, how many will there be in 7 hours?

Let's get a little trickier...

If we start with 200 alien amoebas and each amoeba splits into 1.7 amoebas every 12 hours, how many amoebas will there be in a week?

Set it up and think!

split factor = 1.7

initial population = 200

number of splits = ?

Our split factor is for 12 hours...
There are 14 chunks of these in 7 days...

number of splits = 14

number of amoebas $= 200 \cdot 1.7^{14} \approx 336,755.65$

Your turn!

If we start with 30 alien amoebas and each amoeba splits into 1.15 amoebas every minute, how many amoebas will there be in an hour and a half?

Here's how I'd like for you to remember this formula:

$$\text{number of amoebas} = \left(\text{initial population}\right) \cdot \left(\text{split factor}\right)^{\#}$$

where # = number of splits

* I don't want you to memorize this thing with a t up here.

t usually stands for "time". In the next sections, we'll have years, days and hours-- and these will <u>not</u> always represent the number of splits! You'll see.

Exponentials - Compound Interest

First, we need to understand how compound interest works. It's how your money grows! Getting this will help you understand the best way to save and invest. Yes, it's math... But, not the math of text books... This is the real stuff and it's very simple.

Let's invest $1.00 in an account that pays 12% interest each year... and let's say that the account is compounded yearly.

> Compounded yearly means that, at the end of each year, they add the yearly interest, (12%) to your account. (That's 12% of the amount in your account.

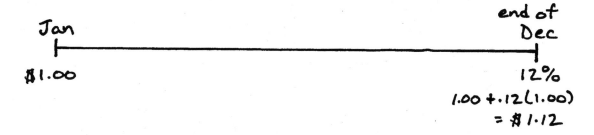

What if we make the same investment, but it's compounded semi-annually?

Compound Interest

Compounded semi-annually
(twice a year) means that, at
the end of June, they add 6%
of the amount in your account...
and at the end of December,
they add another 6%.

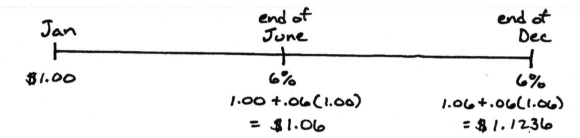

Jan   end of June   end of Dec

$1.00   6%   6%

$$1.00 + .06(1.00) = \$1.06$$

$$1.06 + .06(1.06) = \$1.1236$$

Now, let's make it quarterly...

Compounded quarterly (four times
a year) means that, at the end of
each quarter (three months),
they'll add 3% to your account.
(Remember that this is 3% of what's
in the account at that time.

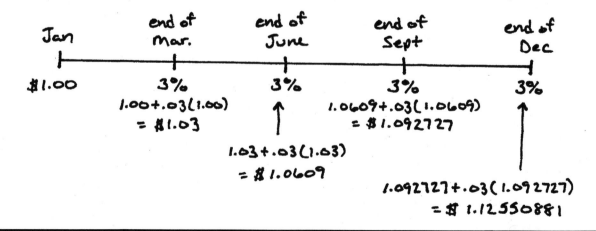

Jan   end of Mar.   end of June   end of Sept   end of Dec

$1.00   3%   3%   3%   3%

$$1.00 + .03(1.00) = \$1.03$$

$$1.03 + .03(1.03) = \$1.0609$$

$$1.0609 + .03(1.0609) = \$1.092727$$

$$1.092727 + .03(1.092727) = \$1.12550881$$

Do you see that, the more times the account is compounded, the more money we make? Sure, it's only a really small increase, but, if we invest a million dollars... Then, it's going to make a big difference!

OK, so how can we figure out compound interest without having to go through each little step? If we had invested that dollar for 20 years, that little chart thing would have been a real pain!

The answer is: SPLIT FACTOR!

Compounded money grows the same way alien amoebas grow! But, since it's money, it'll make more sense to call it the "growth factor."

Let's test it on the last one we figured out:

If we invest $1.00 in an account that pays 12% compounded quarterly, how much will we have in the account at the end of one year?

initial amount = $1.00

At the end of each period (quarter), we'll be earning 3%...

So, each $1.00 will turn into $1.03...

growth factor = $1.03

number of periods = 4

Here's the formula:

$$\text{final amount} = \text{initial amount} \cdot \left(\text{growth factor}\right)^{\text{number of periods}}$$

So, with our numbers:

$$\text{final amount} = 1.00 \, (1.03)^4$$

$$= \$1.12550881$$

Hey, it works! We got the same amount that we got doing it the long way... And this was a LOT easier.

Let's try something messier:

If we invest $20,000 in an account that pays 8% compounded semi-annually, how much will be in the account in 15 years?

$$\text{initial amount} = 20,000$$

At the end of each period (six months), we'll be earning 4%...

So, each $1.00 will turn into $1.04...

$$\text{growth factor} = \$1.04$$

$$\text{number of periods} = 30$$

(That's twice a year for 15 years.)

$$\text{final amount} = 20000 \, (1.04)^{30}$$

$$= \$64,867.95$$

(I rounded it to two places, since it's money.)

Try it!

You invest $60,000 in an account that pays 9% compounded semi-annually. How much will you have in your account in 25 years?

What if we made the same investment, but compounded it quarterly?

initial amount = 20,000

At the end of each period (every 3 months), we'll be earning 2.25%... (That's 9% divided by 4 → .09/4 = .0225)

So, each $1.00 will turn into $1.0225

growth factor = $1.0225

number of periods = 100

$$\text{final amount} = 60000(1.0225)^{100}$$

$$= \$555,242.78$$

See how we made more money? Will we make even more if we compound it monthly?

initial amount = 60,000

At the end of each period (every month), we'll be earning 0.75% (That's 9% divided by $12 \rightarrow .09/12$)

So, each $1.00 will turn into $1.0075...

growth factor = $1.0075

number of periods = 300

$$\text{final amount} = 60000(1.0075)^{300}$$

$$= \$564,504.87$$

So, the more times we compound, the more money we make!! Cool.

Most standard savings accounts compound quarterly... But, some investments, like certificates of deposit (CD's) DO compound monthly.

But, there's one trick to this... Banks can compound as often (or not often) as they like and they won't tell you how they're doing it -- UNLESS YOU ASK! It won't make a lot of difference unless you have a big chunk of money... But, crunch these numbers and figure out which is the best investment:

① Invest $1000 at 3% compounded yearly (just once a year) for 10 years:

② Invest $1000 at a lower rate, 2.98%, compounded monthly for 10 years:

Sure, it's only a few bucks, but every penny counts in the long run! Which one was the better choice?

Compute the same investments, but make it $100,000 for 45 years... Which is the better choice?

Your turn:

If you invest $1,000,000 in an account paying 12%, how much will you have after 20 years if the account is compounded:

Yearly?

Semi-annually?

Quarterly?

Monthly?

Many people change jobs in their late 20's or early 30's ... And the biggest mistake they make is to cash in their company's retirement fund when they leave! It is very tempting ... 10,000 bucks ... just sitting there ... and it's all yours ...

But, what a relatively small amount of money can do for you, if you just leave it alone, is amazing!

Let's say you invest $5000 at age 25 ... at 10% compound monthly ... and walk away ...

Check it out:

age 25:	$5000		age 42:	$38,065.39
age 26:	$5634.13		age 43:	$42,893.03
age 27:	$6348.67		age 44:	$48,332.94
age 28:	$7153.84		age 45:	$54,462.77
age 29:	$8061.13		age 46:	$61,370.01
age 30:	$9083.48		age 47:	$69,153.26
age 31:	$10,235.50		age 48:	$77,923.63
age 32:	$11,533.61		age 49:	$87,806.30
age 33:	$12,996.36		age 50:	$98,942.33
age 34:	$14,644.63		age 51:	$111,490.70
age 35:	$16,501.93		age 52:	$125,630.51
age 36:	$18,594.79		age 53:	$141,563.60
age 37:	$20,963.08		age 54:	$159,517.41
age 38:	$23,610.45		age 55:	$179,748.21
age 39:	$26,604.85		age 56:	$202,544.78
age 40:	$29,979.01		age 57:	$228,232.53
age 41:	$33,781.10		age 58:	$257,178.12
			age 59:	$289,794.75
			age 60:	$326,547.97

Keep reading!

age 61: $367,962.43
age 62: $414,629.28
age 63: $467,214.65
age 64: $526,469.16
age 65: $593,238.63
DANG!

Here's another huge incentive for you to leave it alone: If you take it out early (before you're 59½), you'll have to pay taxes on it and eat a 10% penalty!! You'll probably only end up with about $6000. Not smart! This ranks right up there with the biggest bozo financial moves people make.

For you skeptics out there who are saying, "Yeah, well, $593,238.63 isn't going to be worth that much then."

True, it won't be worth as much as $600K is worth today, but it's still a lot. If we assume a 3.3% inflation factor, that money is still worth $154,984.54 in today's dollars. Five grand turning into something over $150,000 is a pretty good deal.

Exponentials - Continuous Compounding

So, we learned that the more times we compound, the more money we make... What if we could compound continuously?

Let's figure out how the formula for this would work:

We'll invest $1.00 at 100% interest for one year and we'll keep increasing the compounding and see what happens.

A quick example, so you can follow this:

$1.00 compounded quarterly at 100% interest for 1 year...

initial amount = $1

split factor = 1.25

number of splits = 4

final amount = $1 \cdot 1.25^4 \approx \$ 2.4414...$

we can leave this off.

Try it!

Do the same for compounded monthly.

Let's make a table:

TIMES COMPOUNDED	AMOUNT
annually	$2
semi-annually	$2.25
quarterly	≈ $2.4414062...
monthly	≈ $2.6130352...
100 times	≈ $2.7048138...
1000 times	≈ $2.7169239...
10,000	≈ $2.7181459...
100,000	≈ $2.718268...
1,000,000	≈ $2.7182804...

Look at what's happening here. ↑

Not changing very much anymore, are they?
In fact, they are getting closer and closer to a
very special number

$$e \approx 2.7182818...$$

It's an irrational number like π. It goes on
forever and ever and never repeats.

We won't be able to use the split factor for
continuous compounding, but we will be able to
use this e guy... and he came from the split
factor!

Here's our continuous compounding formula:

$$A = P e^{rt} \leftarrow \text{time}$$

final amount $\nearrow$

principle (initial amount) $\nearrow$

interest rate $\searrow$

Let's do an example:

If you invest $1,000,000 in an account paying 12% compounded continuously, how much will you have in the account after 20 years?

$$A = P e^{rt}$$

$$A = 1000000 \, e^{.12(20)} \approx \$11,023,176.38$$

$\uparrow$

This is a button on your calculator!
Look over this button $\boxed{\ln}$.

Compare this to what you got at the end of the last lesson... It should be a decent amount more.

Your turn:

If you invest $25,000 at 7% compounded continuously, how much will you have in 10 years?

Exponentials - Annuities

Annuities are how smart people save! This is where you invest a set amount each month... A little at a time is the way to go!

Here's how it works:

Let's invest $100 each month at 12% compounded monthly...

Beginning of January: You put in $100.

On the last day of January:

They compute your interest...
(Remember that, if we make 12% for the whole year, we'll make 1% each month.)

$$100 + .01(100) = \underline{\$101}$$

On February 1st: You put in another $100.

$$\$101 + \$100 = \underline{\$201}$$

On the last day of February:

They compute your interest...

$$201 + .01(201) = \underline{\$203.01}$$

On March 1st: You put in another $100.

$$\$203.01 + \$100 = \underline{\$303.01}$$

On the last day of March:

They compute your interest...

$303.01 + .01(303.01) = \underline{\$306.0401}$

On April 1st: You put in another $100.

$\$306.0401 + \$100 = \underline{\$406.0401}$

On the last day of April:

They computer your interest...

$406.0401 + .01(406.0401) = \underline{\$410.100501}$

On May 1st: You put in another $100.

$\$410.100501 + \$100 = \underline{\$510.100501}$

On the last day of May:

They computer your interest...

$510.100501 + .01(510.100501) = \underline{\$515.201506}$

On June 1st: You put in another $100.

$\$515.201506 + \$100 = \underline{\$615.201506}$

On the last day of June:

They computer your interest...

$615.201506 + .01(615.201506) = \underline{\$621.3535211}$

On July 1st: You put in another $100.

$621.3535211 + $100 = $721.3535211

On the last day of July:

They compute your interest...

721.3535211 + .01(721.3535211) = $728.5670563

On August 1st: You put in another $100.

$728.5670563 + $100 = $828.5670563

On the last day of August:

They compute your interest...

828.5670563 + .01(828.5670563) = $836.8527268

On September 1st: You put in another $100.

$936.8527268

On the last day of September:

They computer your interest...

$946.2212541

On October 1st: You put in another $100.

$1046.2212541

On the last day of October: Interest

$1056.683467

On November 1ST: Another $100

   $1156.683467

On the last day of November: Interest

   $1168.250301

On December 1ST: Another $100

   $1268.250301

On the last day of December : Interest

   $1280.932804

So, if you invest $100 at the beginning of each month at 12% compounded monthly, at the end of the year, you'll have $1280.93. Your total interest earning is $80.93.

With annuities, you invest a little at a time. We invested a total of $1200.

Let's compare this to a one-time investment like the one's we did in the last section:

If we make a one-time investment of $1200 at 12% compounded monthly, how much will we have at the end of one year?

   Remember the formula:

$$\text{final amount} = \text{initial amount} \cdot \left(\text{growth factor}\right)^{\text{number of periods}}$$

initial amount = $1200

At the end of each period (every month), we'll be earning 1% ...

So, each $1.00 will turn into $1.01 ...

growth factor = $1.01

number of periods = 12

$$\text{final amount} = 1200(1.01)^{12}$$

$$= \$1352.19$$

Hey, we made more money! Isn't it better to invest a little at a time?

The reason we made more money is that the $1200 went in at the BEGINNING of the year. So, the balance was higher the whole year.

BIGGER BALANCE = MORE INTEREST

But, the realistic question is: Would you HAVE the whole $1200 at the beginning of the year? If the answer is "yes," then invest the whole thing. If the answer is "no," then do it a little at a time. This is usually easier for most people.

If the amount you want to invest is realistic for you (like only $100 a month as opposed to a chunk of $1200), then you are far more likely to invest it!

By the way, the term "annuity" is used when something pays you a little each month too. It works both ways.

Luckily, yes, there IS a formula for finding the value of annuity investments!

Note: We are making our investments at the beginning of each period (month in most cases.) The typical annuity formula that appears in some Algebra books is for when the investment is made at the end of the period. This causes the first month's interest to be lost and isn't representative of how most people invest.

Let's invest $100 each month at 12%*. How much will we have in one year?

* If we invest each month, we need to assume that the account will be compounded monthly to use this formula.

Again, we'll use the "growth factor" of money.

investment amount = $100
growth factor = $1.01
interest per period = .01
number of periods = 12

Here's the formula:

$$\text{final amount} = \text{investment amount} \cdot \left(\frac{\text{growth factor}^{\text{number of periods}} - 1}{\text{interest per period}} \right) \cdot \text{growth factor}$$

With our numbers:

$$\text{final amount} = 100 \cdot \left(\frac{1.01^{12} - 1}{.01} \right) \cdot 1.01$$

$$= 1280.932804$$

$$= \$1280.93$$

Hey, it works! We got the same amount that we got doing it the long month-by-month way.

Let's try something messier:

If we invest $400 a month at 8.4%, how much will we have in 40 years?

investment amount = $400
growth factor = $1.007

$$\text{interest per period} = .007$$
$$\text{number of periods} = 480$$

$$\text{final amount} = 400 \cdot \left(\frac{1.007^{480} - 1}{.007} \right) \cdot 1.007$$

$$= \$1,579,791.17$$

Try it:

Invest $250 a month at 9%. How much will you have in 20 years?

---

one more... and this one we'll do yearly instead of monthly. (So, we'll have to assume it's compounded yearly.)

If we invest $5000 a year at 10%, how much will we have in 25 years?

$$\text{investment amount} = \$5000$$
$$\text{growth factor} = \$1.10$$
$$\text{interest per period} = .10$$

number of periods = 25

$$\text{final amount} = 5000 \cdot \left(\frac{1.10^{25} - 1}{.10} \right) \cdot 1.10$$

$$= \$540,908.83$$

Your turn:

Invest $10,000 a year at 15%. How much will you have in 35 years?

Let's say that you want to have over $3,700,000 when you retire at age 65... Which would you rather have to save?

$48,000   or $242,400

There are WAY to many numbers for me to write it all out by hand -- see the website for the rest of this lesson. My hand hurts!

I've got it over at my Finance FREAK site:

http://www.financefreak.com/2-math-2-annuities-3-magic.html

Exponentials - Population Growth

It's probably occurred to you by now that no banks ever have accounts that compound continuously. They're too smart for that! OK, so money really never grows continuously... But, animal populations do! That goes for people, animals and bacteria. (Yes, there is some overlapping there.)

So, here's the formula for population growth (I'm just going to change the letters a little):

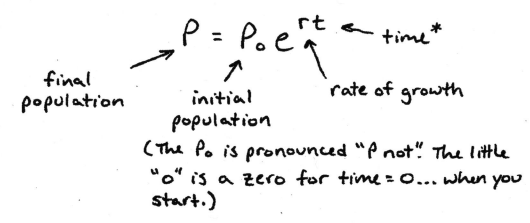

$$P = P_0 e^{rt}$$

final population

initial population

rate of growth

time*

(The P_0 is pronounced "P not". The little "o" is a zero for time = 0... when you start.)

* time is usually in hours or years

Let's just do one -- they're really easy!

In 1950, the world's population was 2,555,982,611. With a growth rate of approximately 1.68%, what was the population in 1955?

First, let's figure out what everything is:

$$P_0 = 2,555,982,611 \qquad r = 1.68\% = .0168 \qquad t = 5$$

$$P = P_0\, e^{rt} = 2555982611\, e^{.0168(5)} \approx 2,779,960,539.8$$

Let's ignore the decimal part since it's not a full person.

So, our guess is that the world's population in 1955 was 2,779,960,539.

(The actual population was 2,780,296,616 so we were pretty close.)

We'll be doing more with populations after I've taught you some more stuff.

Your turn:

At 5pm, you count 26,300 alien bacteria in your petrie dish. If the growth rate is 2.7%, how many bacteria will there be at midnight?

Exponentials - Graphs of Exponentials

It's time to find out what these exponential things look like.

A few lessons ago, we found that the growth of a monster was described by

$$h(t) = 2^t$$

Let's graph it!

To make it easier, let's graph

$$y = 2^x \quad \text{(since we're used to } (x,y) \text{ guys)}$$

Well, when we have no idea what something looks like... we have to plot points:

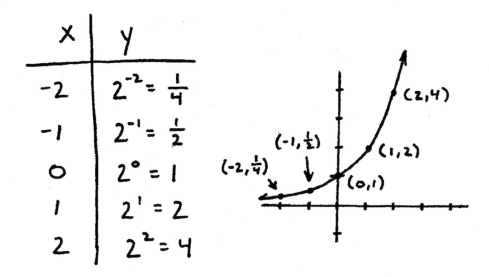

x	y
-2	$2^{-2} = \frac{1}{4}$
-1	$2^{-1} = \frac{1}{2}$
0	$2^0 = 1$
1	$2^1 = 2$
2	$2^2 = 4$

This is the basic shape of an exponential:

$$y = a^x \quad \text{where } a > 1$$

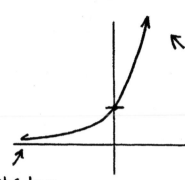

↖ The bigger x gets, the faster it climbs.

← y=0 is a horizontal asymptote.

↗ Graphs hug asymptotes (they get closer and closer and never touch.)

This is called "exponential growth."

What would the graph of this thing look like?

$$y = 2^{-x}$$

Let's see...

This is called "exponential decay."

X	Y
-2	$2^{-(-2)} = 2^2 = 4$
-1	$2^{-(-1)} = 2^1 = 2$
0	$2^{-0} = 1$
1	$2^{-1} = \frac{1}{2}$
2	$2^{-2} = \frac{1}{4}$

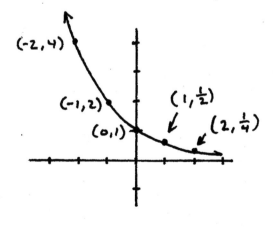

(-2,4)

(-1,2)

(0,1)

$(1, \frac{1}{2})$

$(2, \frac{1}{4})$

I've got some pretty cool examples of exponential decay for later.

Try it!

Graph $y = 3^x$ | Graph $y = 3^{-x}$

Graph $y = \left(\frac{1}{3}\right)^x$ | Graph $y = \left(\frac{1}{3}\right)^{-x}$

Logarithms - What's a Logarithm?

Most simply put, logarithms are inverses of exponentials.

Check it out:

Let's graph the inverse of

$$y = 2^x$$

Remember that every (x,y) has a (y,x) partner, so we'll graph this guy... then nail his inverse!

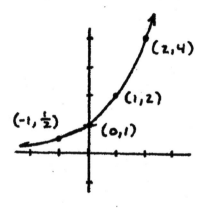

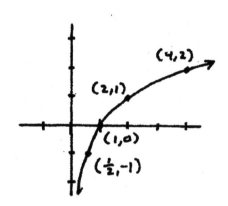

This is the inverse of
$$y = 2^x$$

Remember the steps to find the inverse of a function using algebra? In one part, you switch the x and the y -- right?

So, we could say that the inverse of

$$y = 2^x \text{ is } x = 2^y \ldots$$

But... ya know... in math, we really like to write things like

$$y = x \text{ stuff}$$

So, instead of writing

$$x = 2^Y$$

we give it a special inverse name:

$$y = \log_2 x$$

So, the inverse of $y = 2^x$ is $y = \log_2 x$!

Remember that the base of our exponential guy is 2:

$$y = 2^x$$
$$\quad\quad \nwarrow \text{base}$$

So, the base of the corresponding logarithm is 2:

$$y = \log_2 x$$
$$\quad\quad \nwarrow \text{base}$$

(read as "log to the base 2 of x.")

That's it! Logarithms are just inverses of exponentials!

So... what's the inverse of this?

$$y = 3^x$$

Easy!

The inverse of $y = 3^x$ is $y = \log_3 x$.

But, can you graph it?

I'll get you started, then you can finish it off:

We just graph $y = 3^x$ ... then switch the x's and y's to graph the inverse!

For $y = 3^x$

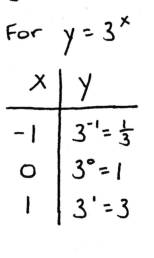

X	Y
-1	$3^{-1} = \frac{1}{3}$
0	$3^0 = 1$
1	$3^1 = 3$

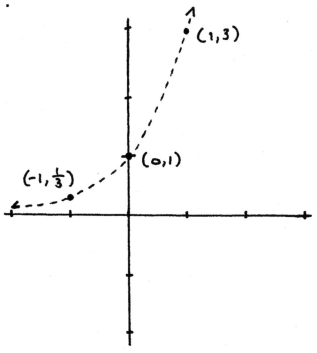

Your turn!

Graph $y = \log_4 x$

Logarithms - Some Special Logs

Here's a special exponential that I haven't told you about yet:

$$y = 10^x$$

He's got a special inverse too...

$$y = \log_{10} x$$

This log turns up so much (biology, chemistry, geology, sound engineering and more), it's called "the common log." It even has its own button on your calculator!

$$\boxed{LOG}$$

See it? Notice that they leave the base, 10, off? It's because this is the most commonly used log, so the 10 is just assumed. From now on, when you see

$$y = \log x, \text{ it's really } y = \log_{10} x.$$

(Just like you leave the 2 off the square root...

$$\sqrt[2]{x} = \sqrt{x} \;)$$

Let's review the graph of $y = 10^x$:

X	Y
-1	$\frac{1}{10}$
0	1
1	10

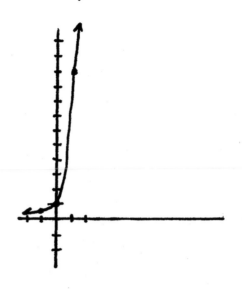

Now, you can graph his inverse, $y = \log x$:

* Remember to switch the x's and y's!

$y = \log x$

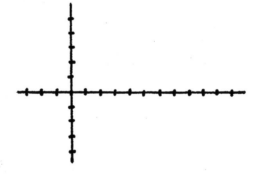

Here's another one:

You've seen by now that this is a very special guy...

$$y = e^x$$

Here's his graph (grab a calculator!):

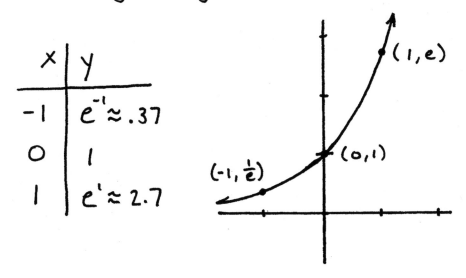

x	y
-1	$e^{-1} \approx .37$
0	1
1	$e^1 \approx 2.7$

(1,e)

(-1, $\frac{1}{e}$)

(0,1)

He's got a very special inverse too...

$$y = \log_e x$$

In fact, he's so special that he gets his own log name and button on your calculator :

The natural log : $y = Ln\, x$

button : $\boxed{Ln}$ or $\boxed{ln}$

*Notice that his inverse, e^x, is right above him!

So, what's his graph?

$$y = Ln \, x$$

Logarithms - Inverse Tricks

Do you remember what inverse functions do to each other?

$$\text{THEY UNDO EACH OTHER!}$$

So...

$$y = e^x \text{ and } y = \ln x \text{ undo each other!}$$

$$y = 10^x \text{ and } y = \log x \text{ undo each other!}$$

$$y = 5^x \text{ and } y = \log_5 x \text{ undo each other!}$$

Notice that the bases match on all of these.

So, in general,

$$y = a^x \text{ and } y = \log_a x \text{ undo each other!}$$

Why am I putting exclamation points on all of these? Because this is <u>very</u> exciting stuff (and I'm a geek). Just wait until the next section -- we'll be able to solve equations with this stuff!

Here's how you usually see these tricks written:

$$\boxed{① \quad \log_a a^x = x}$$

$$\boxed{② \quad a^{\log_a x} = x}$$

Here are some examples of rule ①:

$$\log_5 5^3 = 3 \qquad \log 10^8 = 8 \qquad \operatorname{Ln} e^4 = 4$$

Try it:

$$\log_7 7^2 = \underline{\quad\quad} \qquad\qquad \log_9 9^6 = \underline{\quad\quad}$$

Here are some examples of rule ②:

$$4^{\log_4 2} = 2 \qquad 10^{\log 6} = 6 \qquad e^{\operatorname{Ln} 3} = 3$$

Try it:

$$5^{\log_5 8} = \underline{\quad\quad} \qquad\qquad 2^{\log_2 9} = \underline{\quad\quad}$$

Exponentials and Logarithms – Solving Exponential Equations

So far, we've been solving equations like

$$2x - 5 = 7 \quad \text{and} \quad x^2 - 3x - 10 = 0$$

(a linear equation)   (a quadratic equation)

But, <u>now</u> the unknown is going to be in the exponent!

Check it out:

$$\text{Solve} \quad 5 = e^{7t}$$

We need a way to get to the t... We <u>have</u> to solve for Mr. t. I pity the fool who can't solve Mr. t! Pity the fool! (Sorry for the lame A-Team joke.)

$$5 = e^{7t}$$

Who is in the way?

$$e!$$

How can we ditch that e? Can you think of anything that will undo it?

The natural log! He's an e killer!

Just remember... anything we do to one side of an equation, we have to do to the other!

So... take the natural log of each side:

$$5 = e^{7t}$$

$$\ln 5 = \ln e^{7t}$$

This... undoes this

$$\ln 5 = 7t$$

$$\frac{\ln 5}{7} = \frac{7t}{7}$$

$$\frac{\ln 5}{7} = t$$

So, $t = \dfrac{\ln 5}{7}$ You can pop this into your calculator...

$$t \approx .2299$$

(Four decimal spots is ok.)

Try it!

Solve $10 = e^{2t}$

What about this one?

$$\text{Solve} \quad 1300 = 100e^{.25t}$$

Before we can zap that e, we need to clear a path... the 100 is in the way! (It's the most common mistake to forget to do this.)

So, get rid of the 100:

$$\frac{1300}{100} = \frac{100e^{.25t}}{100}$$

$$13 = e^{.25t}$$

Now, bring in the e killer!

$$Ln\,13 = Ln\,e^{.25t}$$

$$Ln\,13 = .25t$$

$$t = \frac{Ln\,13}{.25} \approx 10.2598$$

Your turn:

$$\text{Solve} \quad 18 = 2e^{4t}$$

Now that you are getting the idea, what can we do to solve this one?

$$7 = 10^t$$

Well, who can undo a 10^t? $\log_{10}$!

$$7 = 10^t$$
$$\log 7 = \log 10^t$$
$$\log 7 = t$$
$$t \approx .8451$$

Try it:

(I'm throwing a trick in, so be careful to clear the path!)

Solve $\quad 5 = 2 \cdot 10^t$

And, no, you cannot multiply the 2 and the 10!

_____

OK, now here's a tricky one!

Solve $\quad 5 = 3^t$

Think! You know how this works now...

What can undo a 3^t? $\log_3$!

But... we don't have a $\log_3$ button on our calculator! Bummer.

WAIT! The natural log can come to the rescue!

HOW?!

Well, in addition to killing e's, he has one more magical power...

He can move the t out of the exponent!

$$\text{Ln } 3^t \dots \quad \overset{\frown}{\text{Ln } 3^t} = t \text{ Ln } 3$$

OK, repeat after me, "Duuuuuude."

Here's the official rule:

$$\boxed{\log_a X^p = p \log_a X}$$

This works for logs of any base!

Back to our problem:

$$5 = 3^t$$
$$\text{Ln } 5 = \text{Ln } 3^t$$
$$\text{Ln } 5 = t \text{ Ln } 3$$
$$\frac{\text{Ln } 5}{\text{Ln } 3} = t \qquad \text{so } t \approx 1.4650$$

Your turn:

$$2 = 7^t$$

_____

$$15 = 5 \cdot 6^t$$ * clear the path!

Exponentials and Logarithms - Solving for Rates & Times

Now that we know how to solve exponential equations, let's go back to money and populations and solve some harder problems.

How long will it take $3000 to grow to $8500 if it is invested in an account that earns 8% compounded quarterly?

Set it up:

initial amount = 3000

final amount = 8500

split factor = 1.02

(remember that each quarter $1.00 splits into $1.02!)

We are looking for time...
We'll need to get the number of splits, #; then adjust it to years.

$$8500 = 3000 \cdot 1.02^{\#}$$ clear the path!

$$\frac{8500}{3000} = 1.02^{\#}$$

$$\frac{17}{6} = 1.02^{\#}$$ Use Ln to get the t down!

$$Ln\left(\frac{17}{6}\right) = Ln\, 1.02^{\#}$$

$$Ln\left(\frac{17}{6}\right) = \# \cdot Ln\, 1.02$$

$$\frac{Ln\left(\frac{17}{6}\right)}{Ln\ 1.02} = \#$$

grab a calculator

$$\# \approx 52.59 \text{ quarters}$$

That's about 13.15 years. (I divided by 4!)

Let's do another one:

How long will it take \$10,000 to grow to \$200,000 if it is invested at 7.5% compounded continuously?

* Compounded continuously means that we need to use this guy:

$$A = Pe^{rt}$$

$$200,000 = 10,000\ e^{.075t}$$

$$20 = e^{.075t} \qquad \text{kill the } e!$$

$$Ln\ 20 = Ln\ e^{.075t}$$

$$Ln\ 20 = .075t$$

$$\frac{Ln\ 20}{.075} = t$$

$$t \approx 39.9 \text{ years}$$

It will take about 39.9 years for \$10,000 to grow into \$200,000 if it is invested at 7.5% compounded continuously.

Try it!

How long will it take $2000 to grow into $6000 if it is invested at 10% compounded monthly?

How long will it take $5039 to grow into $20,000 if it is invested at 4.6% compounded continuously?

If an alien amoeba splits into 1.7 alien amoebas every day, how long will it take for 1000 alien amoebas to grow into 42,000 alien amoebas?

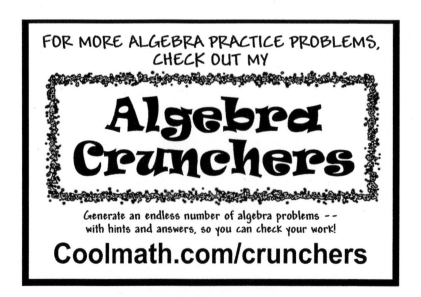

Now for some population stuff:

The world's population in 1950 was 2,555,982,611. In 1970, it was 3,706,601,448. Find the rate of growth.

* Remember our population equation:

$$P = P_0 e^{rt}$$

Set it up:

$$3706601448 = 2555982611 e^{r(20)}$$

$$\frac{3706601448}{2555982611} = e^{20r} \qquad \text{clear the path!}$$

$$Ln\left(\frac{3706601448}{2555982611}\right) = Ln\, e^{20r} \qquad \text{kill the e!}$$

$$Ln\left(\frac{3706601448}{2555982611}\right) = 20r \qquad \text{almost done!}$$

$$\frac{Ln\left(\frac{3706601448}{2555982611}\right)}{20} = r$$

$$r \approx .0185839 \qquad \leftarrow \text{Don't round too much here or you won't be as accurate in this next part!} \swarrow$$

What about predicting?

Can you predict what the world's population will be in 2050?

Let's use the 1950 figure for our P_0:

$$P_0 = 2,555,982,611$$

And we can use the growth rate we just found:

$$r \approx .0185839$$

1950 to 2050 gives us $t = 100$...

$$P = 2555982611\, e^{.0185839(100)}$$

Grab a calculator!

$$P \approx 16,392,546,229$$

So, we predict that there will be 16,392,546,229 people on the earth in 2050.

If you go to www.npg.org, you'll find the table I've been using for my data. They predict that the world's population in 2050 will only be 9,309,051,539!

That's way off our guess. Why were we so far off?

Well, remember the graph of exponential growth?

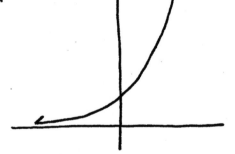

EXPONENTIALS AND LOGARITHMS

It turns out that, in the long run, populations don't really grow exponentially. Because of other factors like disease, war and limited resources, population growth starts to slow down.

This is called logistic growth.
(And it's got a really messy formula.)

But, lucky for us, exponential growth and our formula is a great short-term predictor (model) for populations. It just doesn't work well for large time spans.

Your turn!

If there are 25,329 alien bacteria in your petrie dish at 6am and 100,000 at 7pm, find the rate of growth.

* Note that this is bacteria -- not alien amoebas!

Use this rate to predict how many alien bacteria will there be at midnight?

Exponentials and Logarithms - More Ways to Use This Stuff

Radioactive Decay:

Ever heard of Plutonium? It's the stuff we use in our nuclear things-- weapons, submarines, etc. Plutonium-239 has a half-life of 24,110 years. "Half-life" means that, if you have 100 pounds of Plutonium-239... In 24,110 years, you'd still have 50 pounds left... In another 24,110 years, you'd still have 25 pounds left. This stuff just won't go away! This is why it is such a big concern when a nuclear submarine sinks... Eventually, the salt water will eat through the steel and release the Plutonium (which, as you know, is quite lethal.) They usually talk about either trying to raise the sub or encase it in concrete where it rests. The last figure I heard was that there are currently eight nuclear subs on our ocean floors. Now that I've completely depressed you... back to the math!

Hey, did you know that you are radioactive? You've got this stuff in you called Carbon-14... It comes from cosmic rays that rain down on the earth (and us) from outer space. (By the way, you are mostly Carbon-12, which is not radioactive. That's why we are called "Carbon-based life forms.)

Scientists use Carbon-14 to make a guess at how old some things are -- things that used to be alive like people, animals, wood and natural cloths. It doesn't work for sea creatures and other things that are under water. Think about it... Cosmic rays can't get through the water.

Anyway, they make an estimate of how much Carbon-14 would have been in the thing when it died... Then they measure how much is left in the specimen when they find it. This is where the half-life comes in... the half-life of Carbon-14 is about 5730 years.

Here's one of the formulas they use:

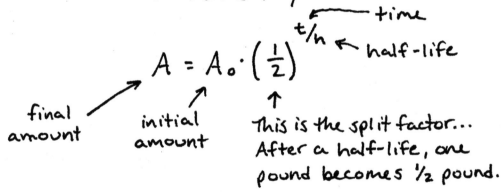

$$A = A_0 \cdot \left(\frac{1}{2}\right)^{t/h}$$

time
half-life

final amount

initial amount

This is the split factor... After a half-life, one pound becomes ½ pound.

If we mess with this a bit, we can make it simpler:

This negative means exponential decay!

$$A = A_0 \cdot 2^{-t/h}$$

You can use either of these formulas. I'm going to use the second one since it's easier and it's used more often.

Let's walk through a problem without the formula first just to make sure that we get the concept of half-life:

In 2000, you buried 15 kg of Carbon-14 in your backyard. Someone digs it up in the year 13,460. How much Carbon-14 did they find?

> OK... That's 11,460 years (which is two half-lives...
>
> After 5730 years, there'd be 7.5 kg.
>
> After 5730 more years, there'd be 3.75 kg.

Now, let's do one with the formula:

You discovered a new radioactive isotope and named it boogonium (don't ask). It's half-life is 1.23 years. If you start with a sample of 45 grams, how much will be left in 6.7 years?

$$A = A_0 \cdot 2^{-t/h}$$

$A_0 = 45 \text{ grams} \quad t = 6.7 \text{ yrs} \quad h = 1.23 \text{ yrs}$

Plug this stuff in!

$$A = 45 \cdot 2^{-6.7/1.23}$$

Grab a calculator!

$$A \approx 1.03 \text{ grams}$$

Your turn:

An alien radioactive isotope has a half-life of 238 years. If you start with a sample of 8 kg, how much will be left in 100 years?

Let's try something a little more complicated...

You are observing a mystery radioactive isotope. At 4 am, there are 2.5 grams and at 9 am, there are 1.7 grams. What's the half-life?

We'll have to solve for h this time!

$$A = A_0 \cdot 2^{-t/h}$$

$$1.7 = 2.5 \cdot 2^{-5/h} \qquad \text{clear the path!}$$

$$\frac{1.7}{2.5} = 2^{-5/h} \qquad \text{How can we get that } h \text{ down?}$$

$$\operatorname{Ln}\left(\frac{1.7}{2.5}\right) = \operatorname{Ln} 2^{-5/h}$$

$$\operatorname{Ln}\left(\frac{1.7}{2.5}\right) = \frac{-5}{h} \cdot \operatorname{Ln} 2$$

OK, we just have to do some more algebra...

$$h \cdot \operatorname{Ln}\left(\frac{1.7}{2.5}\right) = -5 \operatorname{Ln} 2$$

Multiply by h...

$$h = \frac{-5 \operatorname{Ln} 2}{\operatorname{Ln}\left(\frac{1.7}{2.5}\right)} \approx 8.97 \text{ hrs}$$

The half-life is about 8.97 hrs.

Try it!

Doing some digging on an alien planet, you find the bones of a Carbon-based alien life form. If a live alien specimen has 0.7 mg of Carbon-14 in it's bones and you measure 0.2 mg, how old is the specimen?

Decibel Levels:

Here's a chart of some cool decibel levels:

	dB	
	160	
Jet engine - close up		
	150	Snare drums played hard at 6 inches away Trumpet peaks at 5 inches away
	140	Rock singer screaming in microphone (lips on mic)
Threshold of pain		
	130	
Pnuematic (jack) hammer		Cymbal crash
Planes on airport runway	120	
		Fender guitar amplifier, full volume at 10 inches away
Power tools	110	
Subway (not the sandwich shop)	100	
	90	
Heavy truck traffic		
	80	Typical home stereo listening level Acoustic guitar, played with finger at 1 foot away
Average factory		
	70	
Busy street		Small orchestra
	60	Conversational speech at 1 foot away
Average office noise	50	
Quiet conversation	40	
Quiet office	30	
Quiet living room	20	
	10	Quiet recording studio
	0	**Threshold of hearing for healthy youths**

Here's the formula for computing decibel levels:

$$dB = 10 \log \frac{I}{10^{-12}}$$

← intensity of the sound

← intensity of the softest sound a healthy human ear can detect

decibels

* intensity is measured in watts/meter²

Here's an example:

You're at a rock concert and you measure the sound intensity at 100 w/m². Do you need ear plugs?

Well, the threshold of pain is about 130-135 dB...

$$dB = 10 \log \frac{100}{10^{-12}}$$

Put that calculator down! We can do this by hand...

$$= 10 \log \frac{10^2}{10^{-12}} = 10 \log 10^{2-(-12)}$$

$$= 10 \log 10^{14} = 10 \log_{10} 10^{14} = 10 \log_{10} 10^{14}$$

$$= 10 \cdot 14 = 140 \, dB$$

Grab some earplugs!

Your turn: (no calculator!)

You measure the intensity of a sound to be 10,000 w/m². What's the intensity in decibels?

_____

Logarithms – Tricks to Help With Solving Log Equations

This is just a formula game... If you take Calculus, these rules can make impossible problems really easy!

$$① \quad \log_b xy = \log_b x + \log_b y$$

Here's an example that you can double-check on your calculator to see if this really works:

$$\log 10 = \log(2 \cdot 5) = \log 2 + \log 5$$

$$② \quad \log_b\left(\frac{x}{y}\right) = \log_b x - \log_b y$$

Check this on your calculator:

$$\operatorname{Ln} 25 = \operatorname{Ln}\left(\frac{50}{2}\right) = \operatorname{Ln} 50 - \operatorname{Ln} 2$$

Finally, there's our old friend:

$$③ \quad \log_b x^p = p \log_b x$$

Check this on your calculator:

$$\log 9 = \log 3^2 = 2 \log 3$$

Here's how you can use these in Calculus to make your life a lot easier:

Check this guy out:

$$Ln\left(\frac{xwz}{y^2}\right)$$

↑ This is a bit of a mess.

Having logs of little things will be much easier, so let's use our rules:

$$Ln\left(\frac{xwz}{y^2}\right) = Ln(xwz) - Ln\, y^2$$
rule ②

$$= \underbrace{Ln\, x + Ln\, w + Ln\, z}_{\text{rule ①}} - \underset{\text{rule ③}}{2 Ln\, y} \quad \text{Done!}$$

Trust me on this -- the Calculus on this would take about 10 seconds!

Let's do another one:

$$\log\left(\frac{x^2 w}{y z^3}\right) = \log(x^2 w) - \log(y z^3)$$
rule ②

$$= \log x^2 + \log w - (\log y + \log z^3)$$

rule ①   ↑   rule ①

Be careful here!

$$= 2 \log x + \log w - \log y - 3 \log z$$

rule ③   rule ③

I distributed the "−"

It's really easy to just do these guys in your head. Here's how it works:

Guys that start out on the top...

$$\log \left(\frac{x^2 w}{y z^3} \right)$$

end up with "+" signs in front of them:

$$2 \log x + \log w - \log y - 3 \log z$$

+

Guys that start out on the bottom...

$$\log \left(\frac{x^2 w}{y z^3} \right)$$

end up with "-" signs in front of them:

$$2\log x + \log w - \log y - 3\log z$$

Then you just have to deal with the exponents. Easy!

Let's do this guy in one shot:

$$Ln\left(\frac{x^7 w^2}{y^4 z}\right) = 7Ln\, x + 2Ln\, w - 4Ln\, y - Ln\, z$$

Try it!

Rewrite this as a bunch of little logs:

$$\log\left(\frac{z w^8}{y x^6}\right)$$

They only get a little messier...

$$Ln\left(\frac{5x^2 z}{w^3 y^4}\right)^6 = 6Ln\left(\frac{5x^2 z}{w^3 y^4}\right)$$

$$= 6\left[Ln\, 5 + 2Ln\, x + Ln\, z - 3Ln\, w - 4Ln\, y\right]$$

$$= 6Ln\, 5 + 12Ln\, x + 6Ln\, z - 18Ln\, w - 24Ln\, y$$

The only other thing they'll throw at you is roots...
When this happens, just switch over to
exponential notation:

$$\sqrt{x} = x^{\frac{1}{2}}$$

Your turn:

Rewrite this as a bunch of little logs:

$$\log \sqrt{\frac{x \, z^6}{3y^2 w^4}}$$

Logarithms - Solving Log Equations

There are two basic forms for solving logarithmic equations:

    ① $Log(blob) = \#$

    ② $Log(blob) = Log(blob)$

Not every equation will start out in these forms, but you'll be able to use the tricks from the last section to get them there.

With these forms, we'll just need one big thing to finish them off:

<u>The power of inverses!</u>

Let's review for a minute:

What do inverse functions do to each other?

If you don't know that off the top of your head, go back and review that stuff or you're going to be one miserable puppy!

OK, what do inverse functions do to each other?

They undo each other!

Remember that 3^x and $Log_3 x$ are inverses... So, 3^x undoes $Log_3 x$!
Remember that 10^x and $Log\, x$ (really $Log_{10} x$) are inverses... So, 10^x undoes $Log\, x$!
Remember that e^x and $Ln\, x$ (really $Log_e x$) are inverses... So, e^x undoes $Ln\, x$!

Also remember that, whatever you do to one side of an equation, you have to do to the other.

OK, ready to go! Let's start by doing some that are already in the nice forms:

$$Solve \quad Log_2 4x = 3$$

We can't solve anything with this obnoxious Log in here -- he's blocking the x! So... We need to get rid of him. And who can do that?
His inverse!

So... Zap both sides with 2^x!

$$2^{Log_2 4x} = 2^3$$

$$2^{\log_2 4x} = 2^3$$

$$4x = 8 \qquad \text{Now, it's easy!}$$

$$x = 2$$

With that inverse trick, these are really pretty simple.

Let's do some more:

$$\text{Solve } \log 50x = 3$$

Remember that this is really

$$\log_{10} 50x = 3$$

Hit it with the inverse:

$$10^{\log 50x} = 10^3$$

$$10^{\log 50x} = 10^3$$

$$50x = 1000$$

$$x = 20$$

Here's another one that's form #1:

$$\text{Solve } \ln 6x = 5$$

That's the natural log ... Really $\log_e$ ...

Hit it with the inverse!

$$e^{\ln 6x} = e^5$$

$$e^{\ln 6x} = e^5$$

$$6x = e^5 \quad \leftarrow \text{ Leave this guy}$$
the way he is.
He's not as
accurate if you
make him a
decimal!

$$x = \frac{e^5}{6}$$

Your turn:

Solve $\log_3 9x = 4$

_____

Solve $\log(x^2 - 6) = 1$

Now for some form #2 critters:

Solve $\log_5 (x-6) = \log_5 7$

Both sides are logs... But, that's no problem since they are the same base (5).

Hit it with the inverse!

$$5^{\log_5 (x-6)} = 5^{\log_5 7}$$

$$5^{\log_5 (x-6)} = 5^{\log_5 7}$$

$$x - 6 = 7$$

$$x = 13$$

Look back at the original... Easy to see that the answer is 13!

Here's another one:

Solve $\log (x^2 - x) = \log 6$

Zap 'em!

$$10^{\log (x^2 - x)} = 10^{\log 6}$$

$$10^{\log (x^2 - x)} = 10^{\log 6}$$

$$x^2 - x = 6 \qquad \text{one of our old}$$
$$\text{quadratic friends!}$$

$$x^2 - x - 6 = 0$$

$$(x-3)(x+2) = 0$$

$$x - 3 = 0 \quad \text{or} \quad x + 2 = 0$$

$$x = 3 \qquad\qquad x = -2$$

Hey, you know... We'd better start checking our answers to make sure they're OK!

Check $x = 3$: $\text{Log}(x^2 - x) = \text{Log} 6$

$$\text{Log}(3^2 - 3) = \text{Log} 6$$

$$\text{Log} 6 = \text{Log} 6 \quad \text{yep!}$$

Check $x = -2$: $\text{Log}(x^2 - x) = \text{Log} 6$

$$\text{Log}((-2)^2 - (-2)) = \text{Log} 6$$

$$\text{Log}(4 + 2) = \text{Log} 6 \quad \text{yep!}$$

So, in this case, our answers are both good.

One thing you always need to watch out for is an answer that breaks a log's biggest rule:

> You can't take the log of a negative number!

Why not?

Look again at the log's graph:

Logarithms only
exist in positive
x values!

So, Log 0 doesn't exist!
Log(-5) doesn't exist!

Teachers love sneaking these guys in for
answers... So, keep an eye out!

Watch out for x's that give Log 0 too!

Try it:

Solve $Ln(x^2 - 10) = Ln\,3x$

What if the log equations aren't all set up in form #1 or form #2 to zap with the inverse?

No problem! We just use the combining trick from a couple of sections ago.

It's really easy.

Remember that there are two forms to aim for:

① $Log(blob) = \#$

We'll go for this one when there is a term in the equation that's just a number without a log.

② $Log(blob) = Log(blob)$

We'll go for this one when every term in the equation has a log.

Check it out:

Solve $Log_2 3 + Log_2 x = Log_2 5 + Log_2 (x-2)$

Everyone has a log, so it's form #2.

To get it set up, just combine each side:

$$\log_2 3x = \log_2 5(x-2)$$

Now, zap it with the inverse:

$$2^{\log_2 3x} = 2^{\log_2 5(x-2)}$$

$$\cancel{2}^{\log_2 3x} = \cancel{2}^{\log_2 5(x-2)}$$

$$3x = 5(x-2)$$
$$3x = 5x - 10$$
$$-2x = -10$$
$$x = 5$$

What about this guy?

Solve $\quad 2 - \log_5(x-4) = 0$

There's a number without a log...
form #1.

Get the number alone on one side and everything else on the other:

$$2 = \log_5(x-4)$$

Zap it!

$$5^2 = 5^{\log_5(x-4)}$$

$$5^2 = 5^{\log_5 (x-4)}$$
$$25 = x-4$$
$$x = 29$$

Try it:

Solve $\log x^2 + \log 9 = \log 6x$

Solve $\log 4x + 1 = \log (3x+7)$

Freaked out by FRACTIONS?

Then get a quick review at
Coolmath.com/fractions

FOR MORE ALGEBRA PRACTICE PROBLEMS, CHECK OUT MY

Algebra Crunchers

Generate an endless number of algebra problems --
with hints and answers, so you can check your work!

Coolmath.com/crunchers

THE BACK
of the
BOOK

Corrections to this book can be found at

Coolmath.com/oops

(Hopefully, there won't be any!)

If you find a mistake in this book you can also go here to report it to me.
Of course, if you do find a mistake, then that was the part I let my cat write.

pg 36: $a=-3, b=-1, c=-5$
$a=1, b=0, c=-6$

pg 38: all zeros

pg 41: $\{-6, -2\}$

pg 42: $\{3\}$
$\{-\frac{1}{4}, \frac{7}{2}\}$

pg 43: $\{-\frac{3}{4}, 0\}$

pg 44: $\{-5, 5\}$
all zeros

pg 45: $\{-3, 0, 3\}$

pg 46: $\{-3, 0, \frac{1}{2}\}$

pg 48: $\{-3, 6\}$
$\{-17, 10\}$

pg 49: $\{-\frac{1}{2}, 3\}$
$\{-\frac{2}{5}, \frac{3}{2}\}$

pg 50: $\{-2, 0, 2\}$

pg 53: $\{-6, 6\}$

pg 54: $\{-\sqrt{3}, \sqrt{3}\}$

pg 55: $\{-\frac{\sqrt{3}}{2}, \frac{\sqrt{3}}{2}\}$

pg 57: $\{-\frac{23}{4}, \frac{7}{15}\}$
would have factored as
$(15x-7)(4x+23)$

pg 59: $\{\frac{-7-\sqrt{41}}{2}, \frac{-7+\sqrt{41}}{2}\}$
$= \{-6.702, -0.298\}$

pg 60: $\{-\frac{4}{3}, -\frac{2}{5}\}$

pg 61: $\{-\frac{\sqrt{17}}{3}, \frac{\sqrt{17}}{3}\}$

pg 62: $\{\frac{-11-\sqrt{113}}{4}, \frac{-11+\sqrt{113}}{4}\}$
$= \{-5.408, -0.092\}$

pg 63: $\{\frac{5-\sqrt{33}}{2}, \frac{5+\sqrt{33}}{2}\}$
$= \{-0.372, 5.372\}$
$\{-1, 0, 1\}$

pg 64: $\{\frac{-3-\sqrt{6}}{3}, 0, \frac{-3+\sqrt{6}}{3}\}$
$= \{-1.816, -0.184, 0\}$
$\{-\sqrt{7}, \sqrt{7}\}$

pg 69: he squares things

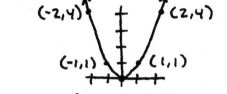

pg 71:

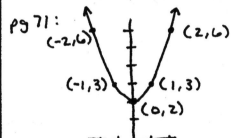

pg 72:

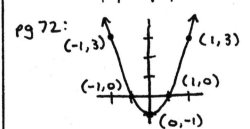

pg 75:

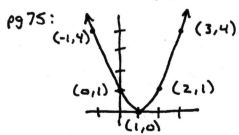

pg 76 :

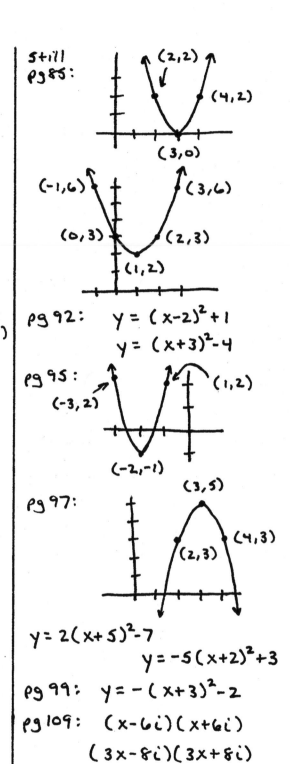

(-5,4) (-1,4)
(-2,1)
(-4,1)
(-3,0)

pg 81 :

(-1,3) (1,3)

(-2,1) (-1,¼) (1,¼) (2,1)

(-1,5) (1,5)

pg 85 :

(-1,-3) (1,-3)

(-3,0) (1,0)
(-2,-3) (0,-3)
(-1,-4)

still
pg 85 :

(2,2) (4,2)
(3,0)

(-1,6) (3,6)
(0,3) (2,3)
(1,2)

pg 92 : $y = (x-2)^2 + 1$
$y = (x+3)^2 - 4$

pg 95 :
(-3,2) (1,2)
(-2,-1)

pg 97 :
(3,5)
(2,3) (4,3)

$y = 2(x+5)^2 - 7$
$y = -5(x+2)^2 + 3$

pg 99 : $y = -(x+3)^2 - 2$

pg 109 : $(x-6i)(x+6i)$
$(3x-8i)(3x+8i)$
$(x-i)(x+i)$

pg 111: $\{5-2i, 5+2i\}$

$\left\{\dfrac{1-\sqrt{111}\,i}{8}, \dfrac{1+\sqrt{111}\,i}{8}\right\}$

pg 112: $\{-9i, 9i\}$

pg 119:

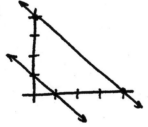

$\leftarrow (2,-3)$

pg 121: $(3,-2)$

pg 122: $(1,-7)$

pg 125: $(15,-8)$

pg 127: $(2,-3)$

pg 129: $(5,-1)$

pg 131: $(1,-6)$

pg 132:

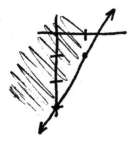

pg 133: Lines are parallel. No solution!

pg 135: Same line. Infinite number of solutions.

pg 137:

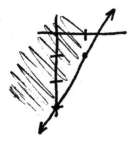

pg 138:

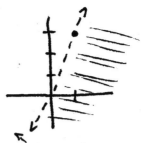

pg 140:

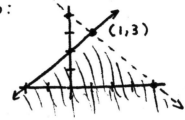

$(1,3)$

pg 142:

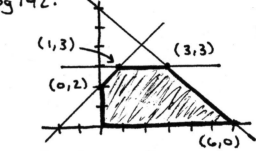

$(1,3)$ $(3,3)$

$(0,2)$

$(6,0)$

pg 149: $(2,3,-5)$

pg 150: $(-4,3,-2)$

pg 155: $(1,-2,0)$

pg 156: $(1,-2,0)$

pg 157: $(4,-2,0)$

pg 163: 14 and 0

pg 165: $\left(\dfrac{1}{46}, \dfrac{197}{92}\right)$

pg 170: -348

pg 174: -137

pg 178: $D=18$, $D_x=9$

$D_y=-18$, $D_z=-99$

$\left(\dfrac{1}{2}, -1, \dfrac{-11}{2}\right)$

pg 188: 16 and 9

pg 189:   0 and 7
    d= $(-\infty,\infty)$ r= $[0,\infty)$
pg 190:   d= $[0,\infty)$ r= $[4,\infty)$
pg 194: $f(x) = 5-x^2$
    $f(0)=5$, $f(6)=-31$,
        $f(-3)=-4$
pg 197:   yes, yes, no
    a vertical line
    no, yes, yes
pg 198:   yes, yes, yes, no
pg 201:   No, since $b\to1$ and $b\to3$.
    Yes, since each element in
    domain goes to exactly one
    element in the range.
pg 207:   d= $(-\infty,\infty)$ r= $[-4,\infty)$
pg 208:   no
    d= $[-2,1]$ r= $[-3,3]$
pg 210: $(-\infty,-7)\cup(-7,\infty)$
pg 211: $(-\infty,-3/5)\cup(-3/5,\infty)$
pg 213: $(-\infty,3]$, $[5/4,\infty)$
pg 216: $4(\text{blob})^2-(\text{blob})$
        $4(x+h)^2-(x+h)$
    $=4x^2+8xh+4h^2-x-h$
pg 219: -3
pg 220: $-6x-3h$
pg 228:

(4,4)
(3,0)
(1,-1)
(-2,-4)
(0,-3)

pg 231: $(\text{blob})^3-6(\text{blob})-5$
        $(g(x))^3-6(g(x))-5$
pg 233: $45x^2-27x+4$
pg 235: $15x^2+3x-1$
    not the same!
pg 239: $(f\circ g)(x) = x$ yes!
    $(f\circ g)(x) = x+5$ no!
pg 241:

    $(f\circ g)(x) = x = (g\circ f)(x)$
pg 243: $f^{-1}(x) = -3/2 x + 15/2$
pg 251:   25.99 ft
        9.19 ft
pg 254:   62.35ft, 403.62ft
    $h(t)=2\cdot5^t$, 771.29cm
pg 256:   70,173 amoebas
pg 257:   8,708,169 amoebas
pg 263: $541,958.18
pg 265: $1343.92
        $1346.66 ← ②
    $378,159.58
    $381,644.64 ← ②
pg 266: $9,646,293.09
        $10,285,717.94
        $10,640,890.56
        $10,892,553.65
pg 269: $2.613
pg 271: $50,343.82
pg 279: $168,224.01

pg 280: $10, 133, 456.80
pg 282:   31,771
pg 285:

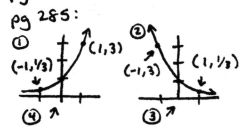

pg 288:

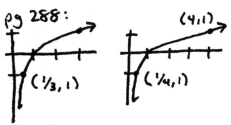

pg 290:

(10,1)

(¹/₁₀, 1)

pg 294: 2, 6, 8, 9
pg 296: $\frac{Ln\,10}{2} \approx 1.1513$
pg 297: $\frac{Ln\,9}{4} \approx .5493$
pg 298: $\log \frac{5}{2} \approx .3979$

pg 300: $\frac{Ln\,2}{Ln\,7} \approx .3562$
         $\frac{Ln\,3}{Ln\,6} \approx .6131$
pg 303: 132.39 mths ≈ 11 years
         29.97 years
pg 304: 7.04 days
pg 307: $r \approx .105632$
pg 308: 169, 580
pg 312: 5.98 kg
pg 313: 10,356 years
pg 316: 160 dB
pg 320:
         $\log z + 8\log w - \log y - 6\log x$
pg 321: $\frac{1}{2}\log x + 3\log z - \frac{1}{2}\log 3$
         $- \log y - 2\log w$
pg 325: $\{9\}$ and $\{-4, 4\}$
pg 328: $\{5\}$
pg 331: $\{\frac{2}{3}\}$ and $\{\frac{7}{37}\}$

Remember that the answers to life's
questions are not in the back of the book!

Are you already in credit card trouble?
Is your FICO score the pits?
Uh... FICO who?
Do you want to learn about this stuff?

Do you want to learn how
to be SMART & RICH?

financeFREAK.com

A fool and his money are soon parted.
Don't be a fool... Be a FREAK!

ARE YOU TOTALLY STRESSED OUT?

You don't have to feel out of control. You don't have to feel nervous. You don't have to feel tired and foggy all the time. Believe me, I've been there myself. I totally remember what it was like to be a student -- and I was a student for a LONG time! Since then, I've been a college teacher so I'm around students all the time - most of them stressed out. Over the years, I've been teaching my students how to de-stress and how to deal with stress... I finally decided to make a stress management site specially designed FOR students -- and anyone else who feels stressed out.

So, settle down and KNOW that you CAN lower your stress! You really ARE in control of what's going on in your world!
YOU CAN ACTUALLY BE HAPPY AND RELAXED -- yeah, even while you're a student!

TotallyStressedOut.com
The stress management site for students